BIPOLAR CHRONICLES:

FROM CRAZED *to* CONTENT

DIANA GRIPPO

All rights reserved. This book or any portion thereof may not be reproduced or used in any manner whatsoever without the express written permission of the publisher except for the use of brief quotations in a book review.

ISBN 978-1-09836-209-6 (print)

ISBN 978-1-09836-210-2 (eBook)

*This book is dedicated to my parents,
whom I love dearly.*

TABLE OF CONTENTS

Prologue 1

Fraternity Party 3

Hello, Psych Ward 10

Sweet Freedom 14

Intersection of Confusion 18

The Flattening 22

Dixie Land 24

ShrinkRap 26

AWOL 30

The Hot Tamale Problem 31

Snappy Dresser 40

San Rafael 43

Vancouver 46

Déjà Vu: Hello Again, Psych Ward 48

Disneyland 50

Back In the Slammer 53

Remember to Floss 55

The Witches of Eastwood 59

Chevy's in Larkspur 61

One Foot In Front Of the Other 63

Back In the Slammer: Part II 65

Student Teaching 66

Here Today, Gone to Maui 67

Campolindo High School and Intel 68

The Cocktail Waitress Body Clock 70

Teach the Children Again 71

Dodged A Bullet 72

Imposter Teacher 73

Hunter S. Thompson In My Head 75

James 80

Alice's Restaurant 85

The Best Luck 94

Thank You, Apple 96

The Wonders of Modern Medication 98

A Spiritual Foundation 100

Dialectical Behavior Therapy 102

Calling All Angels 104

Music Is the Language Of the Soul 108

The List: 109

Resources for Insight: 182

Resources for Support 186

Multicultural Resources for Support 188

Resources for Support in a Crisis 189

PROLOGUE

What follows are my adventures with bipolar disorder. I have been dealing with it for 34 years and have had many up's and down's. It used to be called manic depression, which I find to be a lot more descriptive. Plus, Jimi Hendrix wrote a song called "Manic Depression," and I like that I have something in common with Jimi Hendrix.

Curt Cobain of Nirvana wrote an angry song entitled "Lithium," referencing a drug used to treat bipolar disorder. Sadly, both musicians came to tragic ends, which is often the case for people with bipolar disorder.

The manics are destructive, and the depressions are excruciating.

Bipolar disorder is a chemical imbalance within the brain that is marked by high's and low's. During a manic episode, you feel wired, have a decreased need for sleep, don't eat much, spend or give away a lot of money, and often engage in self-destructive behavior such as substance abuse. Many people with mental illness often have substance abuse problems, as they are self-medicating; sometimes, the substance abuse eclipses the actual illness, and people don't get diagnosed properly. This can be a tragedy with far-reaching consequences.

The depressions, as mentioned, are excruciating. Antidepressants are a no-no for people with bipolar disorder, as they can induce a manic episode. So we are left to deal with our depressions without antidepressants. There are medications to quell the mania, but they are not helpful with the depressions.

I call depression the Black Pit. It is like being in a deep well – impossible to climb out of, and the energy to climb out isn't there. It is going about the day in slow motion, a state devoid of laughter or tears. It is just wanting the pain to end.

I have found, though the years, some coping mechanisms to combat depression and wanted to share them in the hopes that they may help others. I also want to educate people on bipolar disorder so that perhaps family members can spot symptoms and confront a loved one before they are aware of it themselves. It is often difficult to spot symptoms of mania yourself.

I have found The Twelve Steps to be very useful in dealing with depression. It is a spiritual program and has many invaluable exercises such as writing an inventory of people you have harmed and being willing to make amends to them all. I have made many amends to my parents through the years, and we are very close.

Another coping mechanism is music therapy. Music can uplift the spirit and can help, even when you don't feel like listening to it. I list 2,100 songs which can help you feel better. Well, actually, it is 2,099 songs, because I skipped #666 since I am superstitious and didn't think any artist would want to be #666.

Reading spiritually uplifting books and self-help books is very valuable. There is a book called Feeling Good by David D. Burns, M.D. that is incredibly helpful. It talks about the cognitive distortions we have when we are depressed and how to talk back to them.

Another useful coping mechanism is Dialectical Behavior Therapy. It was developed by Marsha Linehan and deals with aspects such as mindfulness and opposite action, behaviors such as exercising when you want to stay in bed, and reaching out when you want to isolate. **It is very difficult to think your way out of a depression, but often your can act your way out of a depression.**

I am wishing that increased understanding of bipolar disorder and coping mechanisms to deal with depression can help you on your journey. And thus, I begin, first, with mania.

FRATERNITY PARTY

I am looking at the Squidly man with tentacles coming out of his sleeves and ink-black hair. He has three Almostletters on his sweatshirt and since I was at UCLA in the Otherlife, I know which fraternity he is in. Fraternities are part of the Powerfake even though the world has decided these are golden boys.

This boy is shrouded in evil, and I need to save him. Some of the dark people need saving and the light needs to stream in and scream in and redeem him. The Voices have told me that I need to jump into the bushes when I see the headlights coming. Even though Light is good, the headlights are MinusGood.

If I keep walking when the darkness comes and I don't stop, this is good for the shrouded people, because they know not of the Light Brigade. I am part of the Light Brigade and it's unfortunate that others of the earth don't understand that I am here to help. Next to the Squidly man is a Barren Heap of Flesh who is so far gone, it is doubtful even I can help him. They both have the same sweatshirt with the same three Almostletters. This is Powerfake in numbers, and I know they are of the Darkness.

The barren heap says to me, "Hey, blondie, what a cute little baglady you are." He obviously has not clued in to the fact that I am here helping the chosen few, of which he is not one.

Barren Heap spews, "What are you doing with that cart? How are you planning on getting any shopping done at three in the mornin, darlin'?" It is so evident he is a Lost One.

"You are a Lost One, and that is damaging, but it is not up to me," I inform him, but alas, this is beyond his comprehension, and he knows nothing but the crucifixion. He knows not of the resurrection. That is

why he does what he does. The Squidly man and the Barren Heap of Flesh are joined by the Un-rinsed One. His hair is dirty and he smells bad. He enters flogging.

"Sweetie, you need some of what we got. C'mon! You guys, we'll take her back to the house, but we should get a preview of coming attractions. Bring her over here." Now Squidly and Barren Heap and Un-rinsed One are grabbing me and telling me to get in.

"I don't need to enter the transportation of the doomed. Doomed I am not."

"Fuck, she's nuts, you guys! This is perfect."

He thinks I have reached the Perfection state, which is complimentary, but not quite accurate, because I am still striving for the Nirvana-mind and have not quite entered in. Now I am sitting in the transportation of the damned in between Barren Heap and Un-rinsed One. Squidly is driving. They are fascinated with the womanly sustenance-givers and are squeezing them thinking they can find sustenance there. But try as they might, there is none. I explain to them that they are not providing food now, that it is a function of a dependent that makes them give milk. They are howling and suckling and trying to still find food, and I am yelling at them that there is no Needful One now, so they are dry, and that is not going to change any time soon.

"Dude, look at that sign and see where we are. We're pretty far out. I think this looks good." They think they are going to achieve Nirvana-mind but they know not that even I am still striving and have not reached. It takes not much scrutinization to realize this.

"Put her in the back of the truck. Man, is it ever dark up here."

Now Un-rinsed One comes and flogs me, and though he knows not what he does, he is still a ghastly one. He will not thrive. His arms are pinning me to the bumpy metal on the bottom of the truck and his Littlebrain is jamming into my thigh. The Littlebrains can make men forget the resurrection and can keep them in the Powerfake. They think they have power with their Littlebrain, but don't they know that we have the power? We don't experience Powerfake because without the obsession of Littlebrain, we think with out hearts. Without me, his Littlebrain would be shrivelized. He needs to know this so I tell him.

Ow. Un-rinsed-ghastly-one is a Violent-maker. I'll need to just keep yelling at him to stop being a violent-maker and to open the gates. There will be a glimmer when he opens the gates.

"You guys, you gotta' come share the love. It's nice and tight in here." He knows not what evil lurks inside of him. I must just keep telling him.

"Shut the fuck up! Can't you just be quiet for two seconds? -Dude, your turn."

"Ow! Fuck! The little bitch kicked me. Take her boots. Throw them in the cab. I can't believe this crazy bitch." His Littlebrain is next and he thinks I should appreciate the fact that his Littlebrain is bigger than Un-rinsed One's Littlebrain. I tell him they are both extremely little Littlebrains. They do not have the intellect to accept this fact and Squidly slaps me harder than Un-rinsed One. I pity their Powerfakes.

All the wars in the name of Littlebrains and Powerfakes. All the hatred that permeates the Powerfakes, and they question it not.

I make sure to keep yelling about the Powerfakes: "Don't you understand that authentic power is exemplified not by violence and intimidation, which is a Powerfake, but by compassion and empathy? You will awaken one day and realize your Powerfakes are in vain. Your Littlebrains will shrivelize and you will realize it is authentic power you yearn for."

"Oh, man, this chick will not shut up, and it's really getting old. She's psycho. I'm outta' here." And Barren Heap didn't even have the guts to enter his Littlebrain. I scared him. Ha! Fear not, Light Brigade. I am here still and their fists were not victorious.

*****

I can't believe they took my shoes. The darkness is winning, and my insides are ruptured from their Littlebrains, and I don't have my shoes. How could the violentmakers have kept my boots? My boots were made for walkin' and I will walk all over their souls. My soles will quiet their souls. It doesn't take much scrutinization to realize that enlightenment enters through the soles and not the head. Or the brain. Why do all those tribal civilizations dance to become closer to the gods? They are not thinking to the gods. They are dancing to them. It is the soles that enlighten the souls.

"Excuse me, Miss! You shouldn't be walking along here." Luckily, I have spotted the headlights in time and have anticipated the shroud of darkness accompanying them. I am safe and no longer seen.

"Where'd you go? Miss? Do you need help?" I am detecting the absence of light from this being.

"Oh, there you are, ma'am. Do you need some help?"

How does he see me? I am safe and no longer seen. He is pretending he sees me. He is tricking me. I will not permit another Littlebrain rupture inside me. Their evilseeds are sprouting in me right now. I will need to find a book on how to kill the evilseeds.

"Ma'am, are you okay?"

"Can't you see? I have no shoes! Obviously, I was doing what any normal person would do under the circumstances. I am walking on the yellow paint because it is softer on my soles, and softer on my soul, and the me that is me, is lost beneath my soul."

"You can't be walking in the middle of the freeway, ma'am. Why don't you just go ahead and get in the car, and tell me where you need to go." He is showing the characteristics of a violent-maker. I will need to fight for my soul. It is time for the end of the Powerfake.

"Ow – ma'am, I'm going to have to ask you to get in the car. Stop. Stop swinging your arms. I'm going to take you down to the station and maybe you can call somebody from there."

He knows not of the resurrection. He is another Littlebrain that has come to spread his evilseed. I will not let him rupture me. No one is permitted. I control the gates. I am the gatekeeper.

"You are not permitted. You have been scrutinized and I have detected the vestiges of danger lurking inside you and I will not permit your Powerfakes – DON'T. YOU. TOUCH. ME. Don't-you-touch-me-don't-you-touch-me-don't-you-touch-me!"

"Ma'am! Stop it! You need help. I'm going to take you down to the station and then we can maybe get you to a hospital –"

"Don't you DARE take me to the Land of the Shuffling. I WILL not go. I will NOT go. I will not GO. Hell, no, we won't go. Hell, no, we won't go. Hell –"

"… mentally unstable – yes, Sir, she – what? No, we haven't arrested her for anything. She did? She is? All right, I'll take her in and we can get her on a 72-hour or something."

"No 72-hour hold. No! I will not go to the Land of the Shuffling. The Land of the Suffering. The Thorazine Shuffle. The Haldol Scuffle. The Seclusion Muffle."

"Apparently, you're in some trouble, ma'am. I talked with another officer who said that a few hours ago, you antagonized some people in a restaurant, ordered hundreds of dollars-worth of food, ate a bit, and then left. You were also said to be using sexually explicit language and were displaying promiscuous behavior. You – "

Explicit-promiscuous-explicit-promiscuous. I guess that deserves the Littlebrain ruptures. I guess it was Hannibal's code and my insides are fertilizing the evil seeds as we speak because it is simply karmic. I see. So it sounds as if you agree with Squidly and Barren Heap of Flesh and the Un-rinsed One. I – "

"Ma'am, you are clearly confused. You need to cooperate. We're on our way to the station, and from there, we're going to take you to County General. There, you can rest, and – "

"Ha! Rest! Rest in restraints! Rest-in-restraints-Rest-in-restraints-Rest – "

"We're here. Be quiet. Get out of the car."

* * * * *

"Hello, officers, I am in trouble because I am explicit and promiscuous and ruptured and soleless. It is, alas, Hannibal's code. I clearly deserve it. Now I am going to go rest in restraints. It is always very restful for me to have my wrists and ankles bound together. Just the thought of it makes me want to drift off into a peaceful reverie…"

* * * * *

There's blood all over these sheets and I think I'm dying.

"Nurse! Doctor! I'm dying! I'm bleeding! Please let me out of these!" I can't believe how screwed they are. Why would they come? They left me here yelling and screaming, so what makes me think they'll somehow have a flood of shiny, happy feelings and come in here? These leather straps around my wrists are digging into my flesh and my skin is all raw from trying to get out of them. I remember last time - I did get out of them. I just have to pretend they're really tight and painful before they're actually that tight, and then I can wriggle out. I've gone AWOL a couple times actually. No better feeling than that. I remember climbing over the fence in one nut house and just walking all night. Freedom.

The straps on my ankles are ripping into my skin and I know I'll be all bruised up again. It smells like pee in here. "Doctor! Come in here!"

No response.

"Someone needs to come into the seclusion room! Someone needs to come in here! Someone please come here! Someone help me! YOU STUPID FUCKS! GET IN HERE!"

Oh-my-god-oh-my-god-oh-my-god. I can't do this again. They can't lock me up in here again. They can't keep me here. They can't put me on a 72-hour hold. They can't. Why do they think they can mess with my destiny? My destiny is not to be locked in a psycho ward for the rest of my life, yet I keep coming back here, and it's been two years, and how long is IT going to last?

They say IT's drugs. I was two years sober when IT happened. I started hearing voices. They said I needed to leave the apartment. They said they had a job for me to do. God had a job for me to do. I sometimes see things and sometimes they're there, and sometimes they're not. I know there's blood on my sheets though. I may be crazy but I'm not stupid. They're not going to come in here. I can scream and cry and thrash and cuss all night and they'll just leave me here. How do these people live with themselves…

* * * * *

"She's out of it. She almost made it out of those restraints and then the Haldol must have kicked in. She's sound asleep now."

"So, Dr., what appears to be the problem?"

"Not a big deal. She appears to be menstruating."

HELLO, PSYCH WARD

I wake up to the sound of yelling. I have to get a tampon. I go out into the hall and see the nurse's station and there's no one there. I wait. The yelling doesn't stop. I can't see where it's coming from. Finally, a plump, chipper brunette in pink scrubs approaches.

"May I have a tampon?" I ask.

"We don't have tampons, only pads."

Disgusting.

"Okay. I'll take one of those. Where's the bathroom?"

"Right down the hall on the left."

"Thanks."

I start down the hall. Now I see where the yelling is coming from. There is a huge, pale young man with pitch-black hair and army fatigues hitting a smaller young man who is skinny, also pale, with light brown hair and a Black Sabbath t-shirt. They are screaming at each other and it sounds like the skinny one stole something from the huge one and the huge one is mad.

They are blocking the bathroom.

I start to turn around when the huge one lunges at me and puts his hands around my neck.

"You gotta' get me outta' here!" he screams.

I'm choking and trying to get some air. I've got to get some air. I didn't make it through a rape only to die in a mental hospital.

Just when I think I'm going to pass out, a large orderly approaches and grabs the pale young man's hands from around my neck. Phew. That was a close one.

After I finish coughing, I say to the pale young man, "I don't work here. There's nothing I can do."

"Oh," he says casually, "I thought you worked here."

I slither into the bathroom and head to the stall. I look between my legs and I am a mess. I grab a pile of toilet paper and go to the sink and wet it. I go back to the stall and get cleaned up.

That's better.

I put on the pad, but I'd chosen to wear a thong so the pad sticks out on both sides and when I pull up the thong the pad sticks to both my thighs.

That's no good.

I pull up my jeans and walk out, pad sticking with every step.

I hear yelling again. It's Todd and the same skinny pale guy. Todd's fist is in the skinny guy's stomach and the skinny guy is making strange noises. The same orderly comes back and grabs Todd and then another bigger orderly comes with a sort of stretcher. The bigger orderly grabs Todd and puts him in four-point restraints.

"Get the fuck off of me!" Todd screams. "What the fuck you doin'?"

"You need to calm down, mister," the bigger orderly says, and gives him a shot.

After that, Todd shuts up.

I know Todd is a ViolentMaker but it is too bad he has to be a victim of the hospital's PowerFakes.

I walk down the hall and into a room with a television. The floor is a vomit-green, the walls are beige, and the chairs are brown with metal legs. There are about five people sitting around the television. Suddenly, I hear,

"Matlock! I want Matlock!"

A woman who must be at least eighty, wearing lime green pants, a turquoise top, and bright white tennis shoes is yelling at the top of her lungs.

"Matlock!"

A red-headed woman says, "Matlock isn't on until 3:00, Edna. You'll have to wait."

"Matlock!"

The red-headed woman sees me standing in the doorway.

"Hi," she says, "I'm Fern. Are you new?"

"Yes, I'm Diana."

"Nice to meet you, Diana."

"Should she be here? I mean, shouldn't she be in some kind of ... home or something?"

"Here husband put her in here. She came after him with a knife. "

"Oh wow."

"Yeah, but who knows what he did, right?

Just then, the nurse comes in.

"Diana, you need to get back to the seclusion room. I only let you out to use the restroom."

"Okay."

I've got to get out of here. Since I'm not in restraints anymore, I'm going to wait until none of the nurses can see me and I'm going to jump on the elevator and I am going to get the hell out of here.

All I have to do is walk the halls for a period of time until someone gets off the elevator. Then I'll get on and I'll be out of here. I make sure to wear my jacket so I'm ready for the cold. I pass the first room on the right. She's in bed. Second room on the right. In bed. First and second rooms on the left: in bed. Third room on the right: he's rocking back and forth in the corner. Third room on the left: The door is closed. I keep tabs on all the rooms and most people are in bed. Pitiful. Doctors' Poison.

SWEET FREEDOM

I hear the elevator and run towards it. Two people are getting out and luckily they look like visitors. I get on very nonchalantly. I push the button for the lobby. No one else gets on. I get out at the lobby and walk slowly out the door. No one sees me. I can't believe it. Could it really be this easy? I turn right out onto the street. Portrero. Is anyone following me? I hide behind a bush just in case. I wait a couple of minutes. No one. Okay! I think I'm free!

I walk for quite a ways without seeing anyone. A few cars pass me and I look down. Then I see a man with a gray beard, gray long hair with a receding hairline, a dirty gray sweatshirt that says "USA," dirty jeans, and brown work boots.

"Hey Blondie," he says.

I don't say anything.

"Hey! I'm talkin' to you!"

He grabs my shoulder, hard.

"I don't want any trouble."

"Then don't ignore me."

"I just got out of the hospital," I say.

"What for?"

"AIDS," I say, and show him my hospital bracelet. Luckily it's on the arm he's not grabbing.

He lets go of my shoulder and walks on.

Wow! I've got to remember that one!

I continue on my way and wish I'd eaten something before I'd left. I'm starving. Before long, the Voices start:

You are alone in this world and always will be.

You are a terrible disappointment.

You are going to hell.

I decide to sing to shut up the Voices.

"Rhiannon rings like a bell through the night, and wouldn't you love to love her…"

I hear a voice from behind me.

"Hey! You sound just like Stevie Nicks!"

I consult Constantine, my Guardian Angel, to see if he's safe. He says yes.

"Thanks!" I answer.

He catches up to me and he is wearing a pink miniskirt, purple top, silver stilettos, and a blonde wig. He (she?) is beautiful.

"Hi," she says in her low voice, "I'm Cherry."

"Hi Cherry, I'm Diana. Nice to meet you."

"It's nice to meet you too. You sound really good."

"Thanks so much."

"What's a nice girl like you doing out here all by herself?"

"I just got out of the hospital."

"What for?"

"I don't know. It's a long story. I'm just glad to be out. What are you doing out here?"

"I just got off work. I'm a dancer. I made huge tips tonight. Want a smoke?"

"Oh yes, thank you so much!"

"I'm getting low. I'm on my way to the liquor store to get more. Wanna' come?"

"Sure."

We walk about five blocks and see the liquor store on the left. We cross the street and head in.

Cherry asks, "If you want a pack of smokes, it's my treat. You probable don't have much money, just getting out of the hospital and all."

"Wow!" I say. "That is so nice! That would be great!"

"What do you smoke?"

"Benson & Hedges Ultra Light Menthol."

"That's a mouthful."

"I know!"

We go to the register and just after the cashier rings up our cigarettes, a group of three young men enter the liquor store. They are all wearing jeans. Two of them have cowboy hats. One of them has a baseball hat. They all have cowboy boots.

One of them with a cowboy hat says, "Well look here, a faggot. How we doin', faggot?"

Cherry looks down at her silver shoes.

"Answer me when I talk to you, faggot!"

"I'm fine," Cherry answers.

"I hate faggots."

"Me too," says the one with the baseball hat.

"I like to beat up on faggots," says the CowboyHatBully.

"Do you have a restroom?" Cherry asks the cashier.

"Yes, it's all the way in the back."

"Thanks!" Cherry says.

"I'll go the restroom too," I say.

Then I say to the three young men, "Leave him alone."

We stayed in the bathrooms for an hour. When we came out, luckily, the guys were gone. We thanked the cashier and went on our way. After a few minutes, Cherry said,

"I'd better get going. My boyfriend's going to wonder where I am."

"Okay," I said, "Thanks for the cigarettes!"

INTERSECTION OF CONFUSION

I'm standing on the corner of Van Ness-and-something. I am protecting the cars from spontaneously combusting. I do this by pointing my Medicine Woman Finger at the drivers before they get to the intersection and then I follow them with my finger until they reach the end of the intersection. The people need to be protected and it is lucky for them that I am here. I've met others in the Light Brigade and they've helped me by letting me borrow blankets at night. It is getting really cold and I forget sometimes where my shopping cart is and have to use the Indian Walking to find it. The Iron Maiden song keeps running through my mind and when the lyrics say, "White man came across the sea; he brought us pain and misery," I am always amazed to look at my skin and see that I am white and that I am part of the pain and misery.

I am embarrassed to be white. I don't understand - The Light Brigade is full of my people who are trying to bring the light to people's attention and cover up the darkness, but the lighter people's skin is, the more darkness it seems lives inside them. And when they see the darkness in other people's skin they are afraid of their own darkness and persecute the darker-skinned people. I have unfair advantages having white skin and having boobs. I know that I would be in jail for things I've done if I were a dark-skinned person and had a penis. I would be locked up without a second chance.

"What are you doing there, Miss?" says a Dark One and I know he is dark because his skin is white and his words give out brown swirly smoke when he speaks.

"I am part of the Light Brigade. I'm helping the people cross the intersection of confusion by pointing clear light at them. All the people I fill up with clear light will know it is their job to save the adolescents who are in the Intersection of Confusion. They are intersecting between childhood and adulthood and we need to fill them with clear light when they enter the Intersection of Confusion."

"That's very interesting. Come over here and explain to my friend what you're doing."

"I have given you enough information and so now you are informed enough to explain to your friend on your own. I do not Double-articulate."

"Double what? What are you talking about?"

"I have spoken and now you know of the Light Brigade and its purpose and the fact that I am one of the founding members and sit on the Board. There is no need for me to explain it again, for now you have the information and can share it with the world." The Dark One's clear light has been eclipsed by the brown smoke and I am not sure he will be able to handle the responsibility. I will need to find a clearer one to help me save the innocent victims of the Intersection of Confusion. My Medicine Woman Finger needs sustenance so I will have to abandon my Savior Responsibilities and get some food.

Zims. I am going to Zims as I have never gotten in trouble there. It is too confusing there for them to keep track of me and what I am eating and when I am leaving. I don't know where my Storage Unit is. Oftentimes, it takes all my energy to perform my Savior Responsibilities and the mundane details such as the whereabouts of a shopping cart elude me. Since I am on the Board of the Light Brigade I see the Big Picture, and it is doubtless I need an Executive Assistant to keep track of such things as carts and blankets and boxes.

Sometimes there are so many boxes and I can find plenty of padding and shelter to save me from the Toxic Floor. If I weren't in a city I would not need to protect myself from the Toxic Floor because I really don't see much concrete in the countryside. But whenever I head for the countryside I am accosted by the Un-Dogs. Un-Dogs of certain breeds no longer have the Happy-Wag. They do not even recognize that I come in peace because their owners have filled them with the brown smoke, and their clear light cannot recognize love and peace anymore, and they are taught to harm and kill. What a pity to take canine creatures of joy and steal their Happy-Wag.

I am now in the Mind-Skipping place where my mind skips and I become confused. I don't remember how to get to Zims so I will just keep walking. Walking and singing. Sing-a-ling and Walkaling… "Supercalifragilisticexpialidocious… Super California Lipstick Extra Salad

Ocean…" Sometimes the voices become Hellyelling and singaling is the thingaling. Music has saved me many-a-time from the Hellyelling in my head.

Music can save me when I sometimes decide that this Hell-on-Earth

has not the worth

and I should exit

the evil earth

and let my Spirit fly in Myrth.

And Van Morrison is telling me to let my Soul and Spirit fly.

"Lady, watch out! What are you doing in the middle of the street, for Chrissake?"

Don't people know anything? I was letting my "Soul and Spirit fly into the Mystic." I am going to quietly slither onto the sidewalk now so my Soul and Spirit don't get Smashed into Smithereens.

"I'm sorry, Ma'am, we're going to need to take you into –"

"Don't touch me! Don't you touch me, Evil One. You are Evil PDBs – "

"PDBs?"

"People Dressed in Blue. Law enforcement agents such as yourselves are PDBs and PowerTrippers and I pity you. Don't you have anything better to do than harass homeless people who have no way to defend themselves? Get away from me. You make me want to vomit.

"HEY! EVERYBODY! I'M BEING HARASSED! I LOOK PRETTY DANGEROUS, DON'T I? AREN'T YOU GLAD THE LAW ENFORCEMENT AGENTS ARE PROTECTING YOU FROM ME? AREN'T YOU GLAD THEY'RE CLEANING UP THE STREETS AND GETTING RID OF HUMAN REFUSE LIKE ME?"

"Alright, lady. Get over here – Hey! Stop it. Stop swinging your arms. Stop – "

"Let GO of me! Stop it! Leave me alone, you PowerTripperFuckers!"

"Lady, you need to come with us. Stop swinging –

Okay, cuff her."

THE FLATTENING

It's happening again. No, please, God, don't let this be happening again.

"Let go of me!" These orderlies are grabbing me and they're hurting me. What are they so afraid of? What is so frightening about me? Why are they hurting me?

"Miss, you are clearly agitated. We need to – "

"You need to what? Do you not see how damaging this is to my Soul? Do you not comprehend that it is you who are Lost Ones? Do you not see?"

They're hurting me and I'm kicking and they won't let me go. Why do they keep doing this to me? And here come the restraints. Those make me crazy, and they would make any sane person crazy. My Soul is dying.

"Stop it! Would you just stop hurting me? I'm not a criminal! God, what is wrong with you people? Why must you treat me like I'm the Devil? What are you so afraid of? Why is there such fear on your faces? Cannot you see that my Envelope has been opened and now my Soul is spilling out? And opening someone's mail is a federal offense! Can you not see that by opening the Envelope my Spirit is swirling? It doesn't know where to go!"

"Ma'am, we need to get you into the hospital and then we can give you something to calm you down. You are not thinking clearly."

Thinking clearly. Thinking clearly? Who can think clearly when you're being grabbed and wrestled and pinned down and tied up in restraints? What are they thinking – are they thinking clearly to treat another Soul this way? Why must it always be turned upside down? Why must the hospitals and the doctors tell me what thinking clearly is? I know what is clear. I know that my Soul is undergoing a Spiritual Emergency, and that it is damaging for my Soul to be treated this way. It is damaging to me and it is damaging to them because they are certainly not going to feel they deserve the Karma that is building. They are just "following orders," but somehow they are going to undergo torture like I am undergoing, whether it happens in this life or another. And they will know not that they are paying for this that they have done unto me.

And perhaps that is it. Perhaps I am simply paying off a Karmic Debt. Perhaps I was a vicious ruler in another life and I tortured people and now I have to pay off this Debt and I am going to have to go from one mental institution to the next for the rest of my life to pay off the Debt. Oh God. Please let this be the last one. I've already been to at least two dozen psych wards. Can I be done with the Debt? Oh, God. What if this is it? What if this is my Destiny and this life is simply a huge Payment? What if I keep going back and back and back to these places and I keep getting tortured and orderlies keep wrestling with me and doctors keep shooting me up with drugs and they all keep telling me I'm just agitated and that this is for my own good…

"Oh, God! Oh, help! Just help - Just come Down Here and do something."

"Hold still, ma'am! Stop it! You need something to calm you down."

"Here - pull those down and give it to her there." And now they might as well be raping me. They're pulling my pants down and I can't do anything about it and I told them not to pull my pants down. And now they are sending poison into me.

Here they come. The drugs. Now all my Real thoughts are going to be swallowed and my mind will enter The Flattening. My Soul will get lost once again beneath the Flattening. It's starting. I can feel my jaw locking and my stomach convulsing because that is what happens when the Doctor's Poison goes into my open Envelope. Who tore open my Envelope and let my Sprit swirl?

DIXIE LAND

"Miss, you need to take your meds. Here you go."

Here I am, back in Dixie Land. The world where they tie your brain in knots by giving you Doctor's Poison in little dixie cups.

My Soul. Where is my Soul? Where is my Spirit? They cannot live in Dixie Land! I must escape Dixie Land! Where is the nearest escape? I have done this before and I'll do it again. I am not going to let my envelope get crumpled and ripped and returned to Sender. My Soul is going to fix the envelope. It is going to fix it from the inside out. It is going to put Cosmic Krazy glue into the gulches. The Cosmic Krazy Glue will win when the Doctor's Poison is swirling in my veins. It will make little rips in my veins for the Poison to leak out and then be transmitted into the Receptacle of Doctor's Poison which in turn will be

eliminated into the toilet. I need to remember water. The water will be the vehicle by which the Doctor's Poison is transmitted into the Receptacle.

"Nurse! I need some more water! Can I please have lots and lots of water?"

This room is white and there is nothing in it except this cot I am on with the four leather straps holding my wrists and ankles. There are holes in each tile of the ceiling and I have counted these before so I know the number to be a consistent 235. There are always 235 holes in the ceiling tiles of mental institutions. That is the law. There is the knowledge that these places are really conceived by the Almost-Devil and instead of being really obvious and making everything 666 which would give it away, the AlmostDevil is more crafty. There is not Devil per se because the angels

Lucifer and Michael and did the Experiment of Time because God told them to. They didn't intend to do anything evil, but when the people of the Earth School Experiment began to believe and worship Time,

Lucifer and Michael tried to fix it. But there was that moment when one thing came before and one thing came after that they couldn't unmake.

We therefore worship time, and the end of Time will be a beauteous thing because it won't be the end of Earth School; it will be the end of the Illusion of Time. So Lucifer and Michael have been helping the people of the Experiment experience everything for the Highest Good, even though there is pain. Earth School doesn't tell its students that. We have to remember. But when we do remember, we know that the AlmostDevil is just Us. We're the people of the Experiment who create Heaven on Earth or Hell on Earth. And that's what they are. There's no literal fire down below. That's a crock of shit. It's so obvious. The fire is below the surface of each Soul and it is up to us to fight the Fire and tame it and wield its power for the force of Good.

So the AlmostDevil has materialized in the form of whomever decides they have other's Best Interest in mind. Because this is an Illusion. To tell someone you're doing something mean or spiteful "because it's for your own good" is an Illusion, and it is not for the Greatest Good. It is the AlmostDevil. It is what makes Capital Punishment. It is what makes War, especially War in the name of God. It is what makes Persecution, and White Supremacy, and Prisons, and Juvenile Detention Centers, and Crucifixion. It is what makes Doctor's Poison … for your own good…

"Ms.… Gripe-o? The doctor would like to see you. I will have some nurses come and take you to his office."

"You mean, you will have some friendly folks come untie me? How lovely. Yes, that would be lovely. I'd love to chat with the doctor." For my own good.

SHRINKRAP

This office is in such stark contrast to the seclusion room that I'm on sensory overload. There is a big mahogany desk with a swivel chair. There is an expensive desk set – the paper-holder matches the pencil-holder and they look like real marble. There is a marble paperweight which makes me think of Jerry Seinfeld and I laugh. ("Where are these people working that they have such great gusts of wind and need weights to hold down their papers…")

"This is a lovely office, Doctor. It's almost as nice as the suite I stayed in last night. Same motif. Marble. Mahogany… "

"Let's see. Your chart says…" These doctors are all the same. No sense of humor. It's like they can't even fathom that a nut-case might say something witty so they pretend they don't even hear. He's fumbling around, flipping through the papers on his clipboard. He has no idea who I am. He's around forty, I'd say, and he has a mustache and beard and probably grew a mustache in the seventies thinking it was really cool, and then he probably grew a beard a little later when he was doing his residency and he wanted to look like Grizzly Adams. He probably wanted to be Grizzly Adams and do a bunch of mountain-man things but is too uncoordinated so he just kept his beard and fantasized that he was a manly man.

He probably hasn't had sex in 2 ½ years and is impotent. He's probably been married twice, once to his high school sweetheart who got bored and left him. Then he married a residency groupie, some student who worshipped him, and she got bored and left him too. He probably masturbates to JC Penny's catalogues and blames his impotency on Deseril. Which is actually pretty accurate since it takes about three days to achieve orgasm on Deseril. So here we are, I can psychoanalyze the heck out of him in three seconds and he is still flipping through my chart like a dumbass and can't even see that I'm a person over here. He's so much more interested in that chart.

That fucking chart. That chart can be your demise. If some orderly is in a bad mood – if you remind him of his ex-girlfriend who cheated on him – he can seriously fuck up your life by saying you displayed certain kinds of behavior. It doesn't matter if it's true or not. It's his word against yours. And you're a nutcase, so who's going to believe you? According to what that chart says, they can inject inordinate amounts of Doctor's Poison into you. They can tie you up in restraints and put you in seclusion for however long they feel like it. It's all up to the chart. It's their Bible. And it's not unlike the fundamentalist interpretation. No room for negotiation. No concept of metaphor or parable. It's written: It's Law.

"So, doctor, what did you find? Can you cure me?"

"Uh, Miss, miss Deborah Gr"

"It's Diana. Diana Grippo. You can look at me. I'm actually breathing over here. I could probably tell you what's going on. I know you're attached to my chart, but – "

"It says in your chart that you've been agitated. It says that when they brought you in, you were shouting obscenities and were generally uncooperative – "

"Doctor, let me ask you something: If you had three large men attacking you and you weren't sure why, and then they began tying you up and shooting you up with drugs, would your first reaction be to cooperate?"

"What I hear you saying is – "

" 'What I hear you saying'? What I hear you saying! Did you actually say that? You are such a cliché. I can't even believe you just said that. Shrinkrap: the language of the upper-class white male who attended some college paid for by said Trust set up by undoubtedly privileged parents.

Did they teach you that in shrink school? How can you possibly think I am going to respect your intelligence when you speak to me in Shrinkrap? How can you possibly expect me to listen to anything you have to say?"

"I hear some agitation in your voice – "

"Can't you think of another damn word? I'm so sick of you people saying I'm agitated. Of course I'm agitated. You don't even give a fuck what's going on with me. All you care about is that chart and the insurance money. You've got a great gig going here. You don't even have to feed nutcases like me, because what can I do? Who will believe me when I tell them I was treated like shit? Who will be on my side? How will I even figure out a way to tell anybody? How will I even be able to get through the red tape to be able to do anything like file a complaint? It's so beyond reprehensible. It's for my own good…"

"Well, yes, Deborah –"

"It's Diana, you moron."

"It is for your own good. You were displaying psychotic behavior and we needed to make sure you weren't a danger to –"

"Oh, like you really give a fuck if I'm a danger to myself or others. First of all, how dangerous am I? Look at me. How much fucking damage could I do to three orderlies attacking me? And I was not a danger to myself. I was having a spritual experience before you assholes came along and administered The Flattening."

"The flattening?"

"Yes, Haldol. Thorazine. Whatever. All of it flattens the emotions and swallows the Soul's voice. You have no idea what I'm talking about but I am not delusional. I am perfectly clear. I am clear and sane and mad. I am so mad. I can't even tell you what little respect I have for you and the other doctors who work in places like this. You don't know jack. You don't know about the Soul."

"It says here in your chart that…"

I can't stay here with this stupidfuck one second longer. I am out of here. I get up and begin to walk out – perfectly calmly – and he pushes the button. I hear people running from down the hall and they are getting closer. My three friends are now standing in front of me, blocking the doorway. Here they are, these bouncers, standing before me, and there's the other one with the needle, and they're all ready to put me back in the restraints, back in seclusion, just because the doctor is a stupidfuck. Oh God. Please come down here.

"LET GO OF ME!"

AWOL

I wake up and feel sort of like me. I try and re-create the past few days. I have a little tiny Honda Civic and all my clothes were in there. But where is it? And when was the last time I saw it? I imagine what my mother is doing right now. She's getting ready for school, planning her day, perhaps teaching Piaget's theory of how toddlers learn language. She teaches psychology. She and my dad are Saints. They are as close to perfect as any two people I have ever met. They drink moderately, don't smoke, and never overeat. They are very kind. They were strict when I was growing up, but in a fair way. I love them so much. I can't be around them right now because I don't want them to see what I've become.

My parents put me in a locked ward for months one time and it was so horrid that I've given a fake name to authorities and doctors ever since. No matter how psychotic I am I can somehow remember to say I'm Chelsea Proscia. And since Chelsea doesn't have insurance, they can't keep her too long.

I decide to call Paul Connor, an eccentric friend of the family's, and tell him I'm in an evil place and since he is like me, he understands that it is an evil place. He is going to come help me escape.

He comes to pick me up.

"You look beautiful," he says.

"Thanks," I reply, but I decide he's kind of a dirty old man so I let him buy me some food at the Good Earth but I'm going to ditch him. I haven't eaten in a lot of days so I finish all the food and then I go to the bathroom and sneak through the kitchen and out the back door of the restaurant.

I need to walk.

THE HOT TAMALE PROBLEM

It all smells like wet cement. Everything. Including me. I'm back in the Tenderloin and I can't find my cart and it had my UCLA diploma in it. I can't keep walking all night in the rain but you can't sleep in this neighborhood at night so I have to keep walking and just wait until daytime to sleep.

I see a young man playing the bongo's and singing in a reggae voice. He is singing along to Bob Marley. He has dreadlocks and is wearing a gray sweatshirt and jeans. He looks up at me. As I listen to Bob Marley, I am trying to feel better but not doing very well.

"You like Bob Marley?" he asks.

"I love Bob Marley," I answer. I'm trying to put on a happy face, but the medicine has made me fall down, down, down.

"Whenever I want to be peaceful, I Marley. I use it as a verb," he explains.

"That's a very interesting idea." I'm trying to be up, but I'm down.

"Come on now, it's not that bad," he says.

"I'm spiraling down. I can feel it and I don't know how to stop it and I need to learn how to stop the Black Pit."

"I know what you need. Let's go to the O. My name's Tyrone, what's yours?" he asks.

Sometimes people call things weird names and I never call them on it because I do it too.

"I'm Diana. Fine, let's go."

We walk a few blocks and it smells like wet cement and urine now. We walk into the O'Farrell Theatre and into the room with the clothes.

"Hey, Abe!"

"Hi, Tyrone. Who's the beautiful lady?"

"This here's BagLadyDi. She needs something pretty."

"Right this way, darlin'."

Abe is one of us. I can tell. We're joined by a beautiful lady wearing a thong. That's it. Her boobs look real. Skinny with big boobs. Good genes. Tyrone is so cute – he's trying not to stare. Abe and the almost-naked-lady lead us upstairs and we go into a room with piles of clothes. I can't wait. There are snakeskin boots and snakeskin pants and leopard print tops and it's *so me*. Who needs a diploma when you can have snakeskin boots and leopard-print clothes? I put on the boots and they're perfect.

"Ever think about dancin'?" asks Abe.

Abe is looking me over and he's so one of us. I start dancing. Sure, I don't just think about it, though. Just do it. And I dance and dance with my happy-feet. I love up. Up and away.

"Tyrone, I need to go to the ATM."

"Now?"

"I want to buy some clothes."

"Yeah, I gotcha'. I'll go with. All right, A, we'll be back."

"Hurry back," Abe says.

And we happy-feet down the stairs and past the other almost-naked-ladies and past the men in a straight line and past the big bouncers at the door.

"Tyrone, don't you think all those tribal people who danced at God were on the right track? God comes through our feet and not our head, don't you think?"

"You're feeling better! You're back, BagLadyDi!"

We walk down O'Farrell and turn on Eddy and we're near Ellis and there's an ATM somewhere and now I'm confused. I'm in the mind-skipping place.

"Tyrone, I forgot where it is."

"Right up here, darlin.'"

We go up to the ATM and I put in my secret number and since I'm in the mind-skipping place maybe that's why it's not working. Is that why? But I put in my secret number again and I can't get the money out and I know there's money in there and it won't come out but I know it's there.

"Fuckin' A! This machine is all fucked up!"

"Try it again, Di."

And I put the card in again and I put in my secret journey and it's not letting me have it and I need clothes and happy-feet and it won't let me and I want to break the machine. I start kicking the machine because it's broken and maybe it's like the vending machine when the Hot Tamales are halfway down and you need to kick it to get the Hot Tamales. And so I keep kicking because I need to get the money for the leopard-print clothes.

"Is there a problem?" And here he is. The fucking power-tripping PDB. I'm so sick of these guys misconstruing my perfectly innocent mishaps and mistaking them for crimes.

"I can't get my money out and I know I have money in there and it's broken!"

I try and calm down but these power-trippers just piss me off.

"Ma'am, I'm sorry but – "

"You are not sorry. You are not sorry at all. You probably have some quota of criminals you're supposed to catch and you're behind on your quota and now you're trying to catch up and you're going to charge me and Tyrone with something you're going to make up and it's not even our fault – " I just can't be calm around these assholes because their vibration is just too low and I click down into their vibration and it's their fault.

"Ma'am, I'm going to have to ask you to – "

"You know what? Would you just cut the bullshit? You're not asking me anything! You power-tripper-fuckers never ask anyone anything but you pretend you do. You're telling us. Can't you just be honest and say I'm-telling-you-that-you're-a-street-person-and-you're-making-others-uncomfortable-by-just-existing. Leave at once so the rich people can feel comfortable. Why can't you just say what you mean and walk your talk, for Chrissake?"

And I'm in the low vibration and I'm yelling but I can't help it they always do this they always make me crazy-low-vibration-yelling-mad.

"Why don't you just leave us be, Officer?"

And that's when it happens. He turns on Tyrone and grabs him and Tyrone didn't do jack to him and I start slamming my fists into that fucker and he-can't-tell-me-and-Tyrone-to-leave and he's low and slow vibration man and he won't let me be up and away.

* * *

Tyrone and I are in the Tenderloin Annex Police Station which is unlike the Pierce Street Annex which is a good place to do the Australian-tourist-with-lost-luggage con on unsuspecting men. But now I can't because I'm here, locked up as if I'm a criminal just because of the Hot Tamale problem with the ATM. Why don't they catch some real criminals instead of just picking on Tyrone and me just because we're up-up-and-away-in-the-beautiful-brain-balloon.

I look at my Vice Watch and it reminds me that I am here to be the watchdog for police corruption and that it is my job to watch the policemen now and catch them at their corruption game.

"This is me, Vagabond Vice, and it's twenty-three-hundred hours and I'm here at the Pierce Street Annex where I'm watching several officers – wait, I'm at the Tenderloin Annex, but I know that's not the name of it..." And now I'm in the mind-skipping place and I can't believe it because

I can't be in the mind-skipping place if I'm supposed to be the watchdog for corruption.

"She's whacked."

"Look at her, she's talking to her bracelet."

"Lemme' see."

"Come over here, check this out – this chick is totally whacked out."

"She's cute."

"She's also psycho."

And now they've decided to let me out! They can tell I'm a danger to them because I am going to expose their corruption and low vibration.

"Yeah, 5150." 5150 means I'm going to the hospital again…

"Cuff her in case."

"Fuck you! Get your hands off me!" And now the power-tripper-fuckers are doing it again and they know I'm dangerous because I'm onto them and they can't get away with this and I need Tyrone to help me Marley.

"Tyrone! Help me Marley!" I've listened to Bob Marley's Legend over and over and over and I know every word on that tape. It makes me more peaceful just to think of the first few notes of Three Little Birds. I'm trying to Marley and sing Three Little Birds or Stir It up or Is This Love but the cuffs are digging into my skin and I have to go to the bathroom and I can't Marley now. They're ruining my Marleying just like they always do.

"Tyrone!"

"You hang in there, Di! I'll meet you back at the O'Farrell Theatre – Ty loves Di – you'll be high… in the sky… by and by… think of me and let your mind fly…" and I hear Tyrone laughing his reggae laugh and I will miss him.

"…5150"

I'm so sick of these 5150's because they don't work. What the fuck. Here I go again.

"Stop it! Get your hands off me!" And I'm here at another hospital and the bouncers are here as if I am evil and dangerous.

"Yeah, she was in county and was hallucinating and freaking people out and we thought we should bring her here."

"I.D.?"

"Nope."

"Go ahead and get the Haldol; she's severely agitated." FUCK! No please no please no please no. I can't. I can't have them feeding my head with the doctor's poison again. It takes so long for the doctor's poison to get out and I can't – " I need them to know that it gives my lockjaw and convulsions and they can't.

"Stop it, Miss! You'll need to be still now. This will calm you down."

NO! YOU DON'T UNDERSTAND! I know this won't calm me down! This will destroy my realthoughts."

"Your real thoughts are psychotic, Ma'am. This will make you feel better."

"No! I know! This won't! This – "

"Yeah, go ahead and pull 'em down and we'll give it to here down there. And the restraints need to be tighter. See how she's hurting herself by flailing around and her wrists and ankles are already getting raw."

"Get me out of these restraints! It's inhumane! It's unconscionable!"

"Ha! We have someone who thinks she's pretty smart, don't we…"

"I'm smarter than you are, asshole." And I try and give him the teacher stare and he's in trouble and he's going to detention. But he just laughs at me.

"Calm down, darlin'! You'll be in la-la-land soon."

"Don't feed my head the poison! Please don't!" And the needle is sticking into me and they have my pants down and they are all looking at me and they're looking at my undies and they're laughing at me and they think they are smarter than me and they're just a bunch of bouncers and they don't know. They don't know that I am sent to report on the corruption here too. And they... and... I'm out.

* * *

I'm in seclusion for the ... huh, I wonder how many times I've been in here? It must be about seventeen by now because I remember the last time I was thinking "Sweet Sixteen." Or was that the time before. I was in Santa Cruz that time and now I'm ... where am I now? Pierce Street Annex. I have to go to the bathroom and the other times they let me pee on myself and this time I don't want to and I want to just go to the bathroom.

"Nurse! I need to go to the bathroom!"

No one's coming. The all-night nurses are always reading or studying or something and they never hear me.

"Nurse! Can I be let out to go to the bathroom?"

Nothing. Shit. I have to do it again. But then I get so cold when I'm all wet. I get shivvery and teeth-clicking. I wish I were at the O doing the happy-feeting. And no one's coming and here I go and it's dribbling now it's gushing now it's warm.

Now it's cold.

I'm so cold. I need to think warm thoughts. I can't think of anything except how I want to put on my snakeskin boots and go back to the O and be with Tyrone and Abe who is one of us I know it. He was agreeing with me about how the All-That-Is comes through our soles. In our feet! And that our souls are in our soles. And he knew what I was talking about and he knew the way my TenFriends know. My TenFriends are my Tenderloin friends and I've met the smartest people on the streets and they are much smarter than the people who work here.

My TenFriends always give me extra blankets even if they don't have hardly anything they give me things and I give them things and the FineDistPeople (the financial district people) never give us anything. The doctors are like the FineDistPeople.

I'm so cold.

And I feel crampy and I've decided that the smell of the hospital gives me my period. Every time I'm in seclusion I get my period. How weird is that? I wonder if I never go into a hospital ever again, maybe I won't get my period anymore? That would be outstanding. I'm going to have to try that experiment. The first thing I have to do is get out of here.

"Help! I'm having my period! Help! Help me! LET ME OUT TO GO TO THE BATHROOM PLEASE!"

"What seems to be the problem here?"

"I'm having my period and I need to go to the bathroom and I have terrible cramps. Can you help me?" It is taking all my self-discipline not to call her a stupid-power-tripping-bitch for ignoring me all fucking night.

"I'll take you to the restroom."

"Thanks." I'm doing it. I'm acting sane. I'm Marleying. I'm able to do this. I can do this.

Just down the hall and … I've been to this one before. There's an exit right around the corner. I am getting the fuck out of here.

"Are there any tampons?"

"There are pads in the restroom."

"Do I have to wear a pad? My undies are all wet because I wet myself and the pad won't stick."

"I'll need to go get an attending to see if there are any tampax."

"Thanks." I need to bite my tongue. She's thinking I'm sane. Malleable. She thinks I'll just go in there and put in the tampon and come out like a good menstrual-minstrel-girl.

"Go ahead," she says.

"I'll just be in the bathroom here." She's believing me, the menstrual-minstrel-manic-mistress… I need to move slowly and not run, because running was how I got caught going AWOL one time.

OK, just slowly slide right out this door… and slowly slide across the floor… Slowly bide my time no more… Slowly ride out of this gore.

Woo-hoo! I'm out! I'm comin' to get you, Tyrone!

SNAPPY DRESSER

I am getting really tired of these clothes. I was so excited to get some good clothes at the O, and I'm really disappointed. I am going to take care of this. I am going to walk until I find a store.

I see a clothing store in the distance, and I am so excited. I walk in, grab six shirts on the hangers; then I grab a leopard-print top and a camouflage top, without the hangers. I go into the dressing room and put on the leopard-print top and the camouflage top underneath my sweatshirt. I walk out slowly, mustn't give myself away…

As I'm walking out the door, two PDB's approach me. Security guards.

"You need to come with us, young lady."

No need to fight. I will just let this happen. We walk around the side of the building and wait.

"What are we waiting for?" I ask.

"The police," one of them answers.

"OK," I say.

The police come, handcuff me, and put me in the back of the squad car. They take me to jail and I'm talking, and I get to the mind-skipping place, and I lose my train of thought.

I can't believe I'm here again. I can't stand this.

"Why don't you catch some real criminals?" I ask.

"People who are hurting other people?" I continue. They are all ignoring me, and I become increasingly mad.

"What's the harm in wanting to be a snappy dresser?" I ask. Still being ignored.

I start to scream and thrash around my cell, until one PDB comes and gets me out.

"She needs to be on a 5150."

Even though this means I'm going to the hospital again, I feel it's been a Victory.

They put me in the squad car and take me to the hospital. I give my fake name, and so since I have no insurance, they won't keep me too long. I'm careful not to act "agitated" anymore so they don't give me the Doctor's Poison. It's working. They don't seem to be preparing any Doctor's Poison for me.

They put me in restraints anyway, since the PDB's tell them I'm "agitated." I'm just going to suck it up, follow all the directions, and get out of here as soon as possible.

I meet with a Chinese doctor named Dr. Chu. He is really smart. Well, all Asians are smart. He tells me I am not schizophrenic, but manic-depressive. He gives me Lithium, and not Haldol or Thorazine, so I don't get lock-jaw, and I don't have convulsions. It makes me feel a bit flat, but I've got to get off this rollercoaster. I'm going to keep taking it if it can remove me from the rollercoaster.

"Can I have something to eat?" I ask a nurse in purple scrubs.

"Lunch is in ten minutes. You can have something then," she answers in a curt voice.

"Thanks," I answer. I am determined not to go down, down, down to the Black Pit.

Lunch is ham sandwiches, and I don't eat meat, so I eat the bread and some Saltine Crackers. The Saltine Crackers taste great.

"Nurse, may I please have some more Saltine Crackers? And maybe some peanut butter?" I ask.

The nurse in the purple scrubs answers, "Let me check and see. You didn't eat your meat."

"I don't eat meat."

"I think we might have some peanut butter. I'll go check after rounds," she says.

"Thanks."

I can't believe it. They haven't put me in seclusion. This is great. I eat my Saltine Crackers and peanut butter. I'm going to not make waves. I'm going to Marley, and I'm going to get out of here and go somewhere beautiful.

I bide my time, and I don't make waves, and I Marley, and I'm out!

I need to walk.

SAN RAFAEL

I walk for a few hours and it feels great. Sweet Freedom! I need to go somewhere beautiful. Angels, take me somewhere beautiful… As I'm walking, I hear a car driving slowly next to me. I look over.

"Hello, are you okay? I see you have a hospital bracelet on, and I just wanted to check and make sure you're alright," a man says. He has a mustache and is probably around forty. He's nice-looking and is driving a pale yellow Mercedes.

"Oh, I'm okay. I just got out of the hospital," I answer.

"I'm sorry to hear that. Listen, I was just heading back to Marin and I could give you a lift if you like."

"That would be great! Thanks! I've never been to Marin but hear it's beautiful."

"Oh yeah, I live in San Rafael and it's really pretty. My name's Kevin, what's yours?"

"I'm Diana. Nice to meet you, Kevin."

"It's nice to meet you too!"

He gets out and opens up the passenger's side door for me. He is about 6'2". We drive and listen to U2. "Where the Streets Have No Name" plays. I wonder if they have street names in San Rafael. I'm on my way to somewhere beautiful! Thank you, Angels!

When we get there, we pull into his driveway and his house is up on a hill. I can see for miles. It is beautiful! The house is really nice, and he gives me a tour. He is a producer, and mostly produces commercials. He has a milk commercial coming up in Vancouver.

"Would you mind if I take a walk?" I ask him. I need to walk. All that time in the car made me really, really need to walk.

"Sure. Knock yourself out. Listen, I'm heading to New George's tonight because Chris Isaak's playing. Would you like to join me?"

"Sure! I love Chris Isaak! Let me take a walk and then I'll be back in time for us to go."

"We can get a bite to eat in downtown San Rafael beforehand," he adds.

"Sounds great! See you later!"

I walk around the neighborhood and stumble upon Dominican University of CA. It has gorgeous buildings and sprawling lawns. *This* is where I'm going to get my Teaching Credential. I sit down on the grass and say a prayer. This is what's going to happen next. I'm going to get my Teaching Credential at Dominican University of CA.

I get back to Kevin's house and tell him my plan.

"That's a great plan!" he exclaims. "How were your grades undergrad?" he asks.

"I had a 3.7," I answer.

"Then you should be able to get a scholarship."

Yes! That's it! I am going to go there tomorrow and apply.

We eat at an Italian Restaurant and I have eggplant Parmesan. It is delicious. This is it. This is a turning point. I have to remember to pray, because that's when things work out.

We go to New George's on Third Street in San Rafael and he drinks Scotch. I have a Vodka Tonic because what's the use in staying sober. I was two years sober when the Voices started so obviously, the Universe didn't reward me for being sober and I may as well have alcohol.

I get buzzed and it feels so, so good to be buzzed. I really have missed this. We dance to Chris Isaak and everything is good.

VANCOUVER

I apply to Dominican University of CA. and am accepted, and get a full scholarship! I start in a few months. Now that I'm feeling stable, I contact my parents so they don't have to see me on the rollercoaster. We go out to dinner and it is so good to see them! They are really excited about Dominican University of CA and I show them all around San Rafael. They say they were so worried about me, that they looked for me. This makes me feel incredibly guilty. I introduce them to Kevin, and they get along really well.

Kevin takes me with him to Vancouver, British Columbia, where he is shooting a milk commercial. It's gorgeous, and all the people he works with are really nice. There's a lot of waiting around when you're shooting a commercial, so I get to know his co-workers pretty well.

I decide to take a bath one night and drink two miniature bottles of Bailey's Irish Cream, but I am too embarrassed to tell Kevin.

"How many bottles of Bailey's did you drink?" he asks me the next morning.

"One," I lie.

"Shit, they charged me for two. I've gotta' take care of that." I feel instant guilt.

I wish I wouldn't have lied. He's such a good guy, I shouldn't lie to him.

It's because I felt guilty that I drank two bottles instead of one that I lied. I just love the feeling of being buzzed. I also use it as medicine, to help me sleep. I started drinking to help me sleep in high school after my shifts at Casa Maria. My parents had no idea. I got wine-in-a-box and would guzzle a glass to get me to sleep. So I wasn't having these fun, drunken experiences. It was medicine. And it works. And I missed it for two years.

How could I go to UCLA and be sober? That was ridiculous and if I had it to do over again, I would have continued to drink my way through college. Insomnia is just too exhausting. And I would have majored in Psychology instead of Economics.

DÉJÀ VU: HELLO AGAIN, PSYCH WARD

Kevin knows I'm crazy but seems to be okay with it. He drinks a lot and we like to drink together, and he lets me smoke in the house, so it's a great deal. I love drinking and smoking. They are just two of life's most joyous gifts. I really missed drinking and being able to fall asleep.

Because I'm having trouble fitting into my skinny jeans, I go on a diet and stop drinking. I run out of my prescription for Lithium, and don't have any refills, and the Voices start.

"You are a fat pig."

"You will never get your Teaching Credential. You're too insane."

I start walking at night because I just have to walk. I can't sleep. I'm returning home from a walk one night when I hear Kevin calling my name, looking for me. He's turning on me. I hide in the bushes because he's turning on me. He doesn't appreciate my ActiveBrain. I hide in the bushes for days but he finds me when I have to stop at a gas station to go number two. I just go number one anywhere, but for number two, I like to use gas stations. I can't believe he's turning on me.

"Diana," he says, "I'm concerned about you. You haven't been sleeping, and I worry about you when you walk all night. I am going to take you to Marin General."

No use fighting.

He takes me to Marin General, and it's nicer here than at most hospitals I have been in. But I get so upset that I'm going to the hospital again that I do fight it. I just can't stop myself. I get angrier and angrier and my body won't calm down and I can't help yelling and thrashing. So I get put in restraints again. And I get put in seclusion again and they shoot me up with Haldol or Thorazine again and I can only stay awake in the fog for a little while, and then, I lose consciousness.

I wake up and decide, it's just not a good place for me to be, these mental institutions. Even if it is in Marin it is filled with crazy people and doctors who give me Doctors' Poison and I can't stay out of the slow-motion fog when they give me the Doctors' Poison.

They let me out of the restraints, and I pretend I want to get some exercise and shoot some hoops because I saw this basketball hoop right by the atrium where we go to smoke. The nurse, whom I counted on to be naïve, was in fact naïve and said sure.

The fence isn't very high. I can do this. I cut up my hands a bit because it is sharp, but I get over. I run through the parking lot and then start walking very calmly when I get to the street. I'm not going to give myself away.

DISNEYLAND

I walk for miles, and I'm getting hungry, so I stop off at the first restaurant I see. It is Sam's Café in Sausalito. I'm sitting down when a guy around thirty comes up to me.

"You mind if I sit with you? You look so lonely."

"Sure," I say.

"My name's Trent. What's yours?"

"Chelsea. It's nice to meet you, Trent." I put on my Australian accent.

"Nice to meet you too. Listen, I have some business at Disneyland and I need someone beautiful to be on my arm to impress the higher-up's. Would you care to join me?"

"Sure!" This is a turn of the tide. I could go for some Pirates of the Caribbean right about now. I haven't been to Disneyland since I was a kid!

"Let's get a bite to eat, and then we can go. Do you want to stop anywhere and get some stuff packed?"

Um, no.

"No, that's OK. I can just get a toothbrush. The only problem is that I'm from Australia and the airport can't find my luggage, so I'm out of luck."

"Your luck just changed! I can get you a toothbrush, no problem. And everything down there will be paid for by my company. So you're good to go."

I eat a salad with salmon, my favorite, and blue cheese dressing.

"I'm a writer," I say, "and I could write an article about Disney's legacy."

"That's a great idea," he says, "How's your salad?"

"Delicious, thank you. Salmon is my favorite."

We get in the car and drive to the airport. We get on the plane and he orders two champagne's.

"Let's celebrate," he says, "to new friendships."

"To new friendships!" I toast. I have to remember to keep my Australian accent.

The flight is only an hour and it is nice and warm when we get off the plane in L.A. We get a rental car and drive to the Disneyland Hotel.

"I'd like to get you something nice to wear since we'll be around all my higher-ups and I want to impress them."

This just gets better and better! We go to a store and I get a silk top and a cardigan and some suede pants. And snakeskin boots to polish them off!

We go to his function and I behave well. It is difficult because I am feeling like I am going down and down, even though things are going so well. I make conversation though, and everything goes fine.

He has some business to take care of, so I decide to go to Disneyland. I am going down and down, though, so I don't have much fun. "It's A Small World, After All" just makes me nostalgic and sad.

I had asked Trent for some money, since I didn't have any, and he gave me some, so I go to the bar. Maybe alcohol will make me feel better.

I order a vodka tonic and drink it as fast as I can.

I remember that part of the reason I stopped drinking was that I was so depressed and alcohol worked in the beginning but then it turned on me and I was depressed again. It helped me sleep but it turned on me. And it's doing it again. It's turning on me. I've headed down to the Black Pit.

I meet Trent back at the hotel and I am in the Black Pit. I'm numb and I'm not the person Trent met, because he liked ManicMe but now I'm not. Now I'm Depressed-Di-who-wants-to-die, and he just didn't sign up for that. I made a list of pro's and con's, and I couldn't go through with anything because on the "con's" side is my parents, and I couldn't do that to them.

"I'm so sorry, Trent, I just am not feeling well, and I don't think I'll be able to stay," I apologize.

"That's okay," he answers, "You were great at my function. Everybody really liked you, and I needed you there. I can get you a plane ticket and you can head back."

Phew.

I get on the plane and try and sleep but I can't. I land at SFO and get some cigarettes. I smoke and think, and think and smoke, and how did I get into the Black Pit again? It must have been the Doctor's Poison.

BACK IN THE SLAMMER

I've been sleeping here at SFO and taking sponge baths in the airport bathroom for awhile, and it's so cold outside, I feel lucky I'm not on the streets. But I used the last of Trent's money on cigarettes, and I eat onion rings and don't pay because I don't have any money, and they catch me and think I'm a vagrant.

So I wrecked it with Kevin and I wrecked it with Trent and I'm back living the life of a bag lady. Because that's justice. I deserve it.

I can't believe it. They throw me out of SFO and I don't even have to go to jail. I tell the police I'm from Australia and the airline lost my luggage, and they let me go. If I were Tyrone, I would have gone to jail. I am aware this isn't fair, and I don't deserve my luck, but I'm not about to tell them this.

I share a cab with an older couple, and I tell them that the airline lost my luggage, and they are nice enough to pay for the cab ride. I reach Market Street and head to Zim's. The onion rings are the only thing I've had in two days and I'm starving.

I get a veggie omelet and it is delectable. I eat very slowly and hope that they get really busy and won't notice when I walk out. I go to the bathroom before I leave, and wash my face. I saunter out the door, and right after I reach the sidewalk, I see a security guard approaching me. Well, I dodged a bullet at SFO but justice has caught up with me.

"You need to come with me, Miss," he says.

"OK," I reply. Can't fight it.

He takes me to the street where the police are waiting. They handcuff me and put me in the squad car.

We get to jail and I'm trying not to act psychotic because frankly, it is safer in here, because they don't put me in restraints, and they don't put me in seclusion, and they don't shoot me up with drugs against my will.

The Voices are getting really loud and Hellyelling in my head so I sing to shut them up. It works for a while, but they are encroaching on my singing and I finally scream at them to stop.

Oops. I didn't know anyone was listening and how could I be so stupid?

An officer with brown hair and a gray mustache approaches the cell.

"Anyone hearing voices is a candidate for a 5150. We're going to take you to a hospital," the officer says.

"Thanks," I say. No use fighting it. At least I won't get a record.

REMEMBER TO FLOSS

I am trying to get comfortable in the seclusion room. My wrists and ankles are still in restraints so it's not like I can scratch the damn itch on my nose. So it's really not comfortable at all, but if I think about it too much, I'll fly into a rage. I'm trying to be as quiet and sane as I can. I am getting better at fooling them. It's only when they surprise me with the grabbing orderlies and the restraints that I can't control myself. Now at least I'm getting better at controlling myself when the hospital staff talks to me like I have shit-for-brains. It's that same old thing – I may be crazy but I'm not stupid.

The floor is of course Toxic Floor. The walls are tiles with holes in them. I guess they don't want you to become attached to the hospital so they make the rooms suck as much as possible. I will have to remember to count the number of holes in the tiles on account of the Devil and everything. I had that all worked out in my mind and now it's getting fuzzy from the Mind Skipping. I hate it when I have epiphanies and don't remember them.

I have my escape all planned. I met two other inmates named Tom and Lindsay. When it's time for meds, Tom is going to have a fake psychotic episode and he's about 250 pounds so that will take up most of the staff. Then, I asked Lindsay if she'd use a pack of dental floss to prop open the atrium door. I did research on various door-propping items. Some items have plastic that is too slippery and the door just slides closed. Some items are too wide and it becomes obvious that the door is being propped open. Some items are too brightly colored, and some had rounded edges and the door would inch closed little by little. After I get out on to the atrium, I can climb over the fence I scouted yesterday. Totally easy fence. Again, they forget that we're crazy and not stupid.

My thinking is clearer today and I am just praying I don't enter the Black Pit. Sometimes when my thinking gets less confused I keep going down and down into DreadLand. It's a place where I dread life and don't want to participate anymore. The thing that's weird is that my thinking may be more linear in DreadLand and therefore more acceptable to authorities of all kinds; but my DreadLand conviction of the meaninglessness of life is totally illogical. At least when I'm manic I believe in a Spiritual EverLand, a place where our Souls were before they were here, and a place where they'll go when we're gone. Why is it so much more socially acceptable to be in DreadLand where we decide that we're here once; shit happens; and then we die. That to me makes absolutely no sense. There is no logic whatsoever in that view. The doctors like it better though.

I am looking at the purple and green bruises on my legs from the restraints. Dangerous places, these hospitals. I wonder how many people know what really goes on here. I wonder how many people know that these places are so under-staffed that when one person gets out of control, they have to sedate that person because keeping the ward as calm as possible is the ultimate goal. So it's all well and good if you're taking a tour of the place or something, and everybody's doing the Thorazine Shuffle (slow motion walking – no arm movement at all.) If you happen to be a *patient* on the ward, God forbid, you are sedated and often restrained at the first sign of agitation. And why can't they at least find three good synonyms for that word?

"Deena, are you feeling less agitated?"

"Yes." I need to keep my answers really short or I will accidentally tell him he is a fuckface.

"I also need to go to the bathroom." Luckily, I've been attended to in the nick of time and I won't have to pee on myself the way I do when they forget about me in the Seclusion Room.

"Can I please have my clothes?"

"Let me look at your chart."

Fuckadeliac. What a freak. He has to look at my chart to see if I'm fit to get dressed. He can't just decide by the way I am acting so calm. In fact, I am so calm I may just implode… He has to look at my fucking chart. I am out of this shit hole. Welcome to the Hotel California….

"Dinah, I checked with the nurse and she says you can have your clothes if you feel you are calm and ready to join the patients on the rest of the ward. Are you calm?"

"Yes." Fuckface.

"Here you are, now I will be right out here and when you are dressed I will escort you to the day room."

I hope I still have those cigarettes in my back pocket. Shit. They took them. I bet mental ward orderlies never have to buy smokes because they steal them all from us. God, I need a cigarette. I need to have something in my body to stave off the impending tantrum I feel coming on. I just cannot stand the way they treat us when we are in these places. If we're not being treated like animals – tied up and caged – we're being treated with such condescension that it becomes clear we are regarded as inferior beings, unfit for the world, and they are the Gatekeepers.

"Nurse! Something's wrong with Tom!" Here we go…

They're all running towards Tom who is having some sort of convulsive fit and yelling about rabies shots. Way to go, Tom. I knew I could count on you. And there's Lindsay. She's so cool. I can't believe she's not going to come with me. She is definitely in DreadLand though and it is hard to be with someone from EverLand when you are in DreadLand. I'm walking very slowly along the walls of the day room and everyone's attention is on Tom. There's the floss. I will have to remember to floss in the future in a ritual of gratitude.

I'm out! I'm out the door and there's the fence and here I go. I can still hear Tom yelling. I hope I see Lindsay and Tom on the outside someday so I can thank them for getting me out of the land of fuckadeliacs.

I am so hungry I can't stand it, and I still need to go to the bathroom.

"Hey, lady, watch out!"

I hate being called lady. I wonder why it sounds so rude. Supposedly, it's a compliment to be a "lady." She "walks like a lady" implies a sort of elegance. Odd.

"Get out of the road, lady!"

I wheel around and decide it's time to set this person straight. "What seems to be the problem?"

"You're in the middle of the road, that's the problem. Get out of the way!" He has really pale skin and his hair has sort of a pompadour thing going. He's leaning out his black Camaro's window and I've decided he's caught in a time warp.

"Perhaps I can help you transport yourself to the eighties. It's a time of conspicuous consumption. You should be in a BMW, and you shouldn't be smoking pot. You should be doing coke. You should have a skinny tie on and shorter hair. You should be listening not to heavy metal but to New Wave. You should be – "

"What the hell are you talking about? You're nuts. Why should I listen to a crazy lady walking in the middle of the street?"

"You bring up a good point. It may appear that I am crazy, but I am truly enlightened, and that is why you may be feeling a bit nervous. I understand. It can be intimidating to be around a person who is more enlightened that you are. It can bring up your insecurities and – "

"Get the FUCK out of the way!" And I decide that it's time for the Light Brigade to steer clear of any more Evil Seeds.

I decide, in a flash of inspiration, to call my parents.

THE WITCHES OF EASTWOOD

My mom answers.

"It happened again," I say.

"Oh honey, I'm so sorry," she replies.

"They keep giving me the wrong medicine. I need Lithium."

"Where are you?" she asks.

"I'm at a gas station on Van Ness."

"Stay there. We're going to come get you and we're going to get you some Lithium."

I tell her the name of the gas station and the nearest cross street, and I thank God for my parents.

We go to a psychiatrist and explain the situation and I get a prescription for Lithium. I take it and though it makes me flat, it makes the Voices go away and helps me sleep.

Since I am going to start Dominican University of CA in a couple months, my parents and I look around for housing and they are going to help me. I am so lucky to have them.

We find two rich sisters living in their parents' house who want some extra cash and don't ask for first and last month's rent. Hallelujah! Their names are Jenny and Sherri. They are both tall, brunette, and beautiful: the polar opposite of me.

They both smoke, so I won't have to go outside for a cigarette. It's my lucky day!

I move in the next week. I've been depressed but am not as bad as I sometimes get. I'm like a zombie but I've done this my whole life so I know how to do it. I know how to be suicidal and live life as though I'm normal. I've done it since I was about twelve and I've got it down. So I pretended I was normal when filling out the Dominican University of CA application, and I pretended I was normal when I met Jenny and Sherry. They call themselves The Witches of Eastwood, like *The Witches of Eastwick*, because they live on Eastwood Road in Larkspur.

And I pretend I'm normal when I get a job at Chevy's in Larkspur as a waitress.

CHEVY'S IN LARKSPUR

Since I've been pretending to be normal and haven't gotten manic in awhile, I'm putting one foot in front of the other and trying to ignore the depression. Right now, I'm doing 300 roll-ups after my shift at Chevy's. It is 2:30 in the morning. Roll-ups are forks, knives, and spoons wrapped into a neat little napkin package, so the busboys can throw them on the tables for the quickest turn-around possible. The busboys are all so nice. They are all Hispanic and are such hard workers.

Everyone who works at Chevy's is nice, especially my manager, Angie. She is one of the kindest people I've ever met. She always has a smile on her face. She is always calm, even when it gets crazy-busy.

Since I loathe mornings and have a strange circadian rhythm, going to bed at 3am doesn't bother me. It's not a normal schedule, but it works for me. It's when I'm finally tired.

Trying to be normal takes a lot of energy, but I think all my co-workers think I'm pretty normal, and I haven't heard whispers of InsaneBlame, so I think I'm pulling it off right now.

I love Marin. I'm so glad I found it in a manic. I love the New Age Bookstores and the beauty and the people. I was hoping I wouldn't be disappointed when I came out of my manic and was living here, but it was a great decision. And I'm still depressed but I can wake up at noon because I get to sleep so late / early.

My parents helped me with the first month's rent, and now I'm making enough at Chevy's to pay rent to the Witches. But now I know why they call themselves the Witches of Eastwood: They have nothing nice to say about anybody. They badmouth all their co-workers; they badmouth their "friends," their parents, celebrities… I'm sure when I walk out of the room they say horrible things about me.

ONE FOOT IN FRONT OF THE OTHER

I figure since I was insane and not medicated, and now I am medicated, now maybe I can drink like a normal person. So I'm trying to do that. I watch people and see how much they're drinking, and match them, and try not to overdo. I've never been a moderate drinker, or a moderate anything, so I don't know how to do this, but I just watch closely.

I'm sleeping again. I love alcohol and cigarettes.

I start classes for my teaching credential at Dominican University of CA and I'm acting like a normal student. I don't think anyone suspects. I meet a girl named Sarah who is really nice. She is having tacos and margaritas at her apartment and asks me to come. She is my first non-psych-ward non-street-person acquaintance in quite a few years, except for the Witches, but they are kind of insane. I will have to work hard so she doesn't suspect. Sarah is down-to-earth and fun and so nice, much nicer than the Witches of Eastwood.

I am pretending to be a normal person waitressing at a restaurant and a normal student taking classes and studying for things and walking around this beautiful place. I am getting straight A's, but I am still operating in UnderWaterPace due to Lithium and everything takes me so long. It takes me so long to wake up after I wake up – three hours or more. It takes me so long to get out the door. It takes me so long to read anything and be able to comprehend what I'm reading. It takes me so long to write papers and do assignments. No wonder I drank through most of college, and no wonder I was so depressed when I stopped.

I think I used to be a pretty social child, not autistic or anything. But now I'm feeling somewhere between autistic and exhausted – Autaustion. I can't seem to get the energy to do anything but go to work, go to class, and go to sleep. I don't have a life and I don't have the energy to build one. I hate Lithium. I hate UnderWaterPace. I hate Autaustion. I'm terrified to go off my meds though because then I'd get psychotic and do something insane and get fired and get kicked out of the credential program and that would be it for me. I have to stay on these meds so I don't end up on the streets or in a mental institution. But I hate Lithium.

I'm just putting one foot in front of the other, trying to keep it together and not let anyone guess that I'm a crazy person. I keep thinking I'll give it away and someone will guess. I miss ManicMe because it was such a relief from being depressed. I miss the high's. But I don't miss being on the streets or being in seclusion or being in restraints and being cold. I was always so cold. I'm living without passion and am not having any fun but I'm living a more normal type of life than I have in a long time.

BACK IN THE SLAMMER: PART II

I get in such a foul mood whenever I go grocery shopping and it finally occurs to me since today is really hot and I'm wearing shorts: It's *freezing* in grocery stores. I hate being freezing. It reminds me of the streets and the psych wards and being confused and being hungry and always being chilled to the bone. I wish I could forget everything that happened and live a normal life and not have stupid hang-ups like GroceryPhobia.

I buy some wine and am so freezing I go home and guzzle it. Oh… That is so much better.

Today is St. Patrick's Day and I go to a party. It's a lot of fun.

As I'm driving home from the St. Patrick's Day party and pulling into our Witches of Eastwood driveway, I see the flashing lights. They give me a sobriety test and I fail, and I get a DUI and spend the night in jail. I barely remember the details. I've blown it and I need to get sober. I will not drink again.

* * *

I miss alcohol. I can't sleep.

I have thirty days sobriety and am just putting one foot in front of the other. I am finished with the first year of the teaching credential program and got straight A's. I'm still working at Chevy's and no one has guessed I'm insane. I miss my reward though because that's how I've done school: study hard and party hard. Although it's not really partying when you're guzzling a glass of wine to fall asleep. I miss it. I miss my reward.

STUDENT TEACHING

I end up having to break up with Kevin because he was my drinking buddy and now that I'm not drinking I realize we have nothing in common. That's what we had in common. I'm starting my student teaching this semester at Redwood High School and Mrs. Johnson is my master teacher. She is a goddess. I did my first lesson on The Cask of Amontillado and I copied one of my Grateful Dead stickers and drew little skeletons on the study guide. She really liked it. The students are being kind to me, and so far, so good.

I'm trying to act like a normal teacher acts and not let them know I'm a veteran inmate. They have no idea I've been in jail and they have no idea I lived on the streets and they have no idea I should probably not be allowed to work with children based on my background. Of course these children are all seventeen and all of them are taller than I am.

I'm wondering how teachers do it because they have a lesson plan for every period, every day, and I just spent six hours on one lesson plan. Thirty-six hours to get ready for one day. That means I'll be making about negative-four dollars an hour. But I'm supposed to do this. I still think about my manic Intersection of Confusion delusion: Adolescence is the intersection between childhood and adulthood, and I am supposed to help save the adolescents.

HERE TODAY, GONE TO MAUI

There are no jobs for high school English teachers. I've looked and looked and there are none. I can substitute but then that means I'll be substituting for a whole year and I won't be a real teacher. I need to be a real teacher.

Mom and I go to Maui for vacation and I fall in love with it and apply to teach there. I get a job at Lahainaluna High School on Maui and I'm going.

* * *

I have a year's sobriety and am the only sober person on this island. I don't know what I was thinking coming here with only a year's sobriety but it's taking all the discipline I have to stay away from alcohol. And people sure party hard on this island paradise.

But I love my students. They are all huge Tongans, Samoans, and Puerto Ricans. I find out that people who are well-off and educated send their kids to private schools in Hawaii, so the public high schools on the islands end up being like inner city schools. I really like these kids. But I don't like my friends that much. They are all mad partiers and drink and get stoned every day, including my roommates.

This is so weird because I am finally not feeling like people are going to guess that I'm crazy. The Lithium still has me on UnderWaterPace, so I have to sleep all weekend. I get up in the morning and the island is asleep because most people work in restaurants, bars, or hotels. I teach all day and love the kids but am the only non-native so I feel like kind of an outsider. When I come home, my roommates and the rest of the people my age have left for work. And I work on my lesson plans, correct papers and fall asleep.

CAMPOLINDO HIGH SCHOOL AND INTEL

I couldn't stay in Hawaii any longer with only one "friend" who ended up being mean. I also feel embarrassed that I was in paradise and wasn't happy. I came back and interviewed at some schools and got a job at Campolindo High School in Moraga, which is a beautiful town.

I meet some really nice people teaching and become friends with a woman named Barb. She is wonderful: really insightful and empathetic. I join a Women's Group which is great.

I still have to sleep all weekend just to "do" life.

I really like my students, and at the end of the year they vote me "Teacher of the Year," so I definitely feel like an imposter.

I last two years and then decide teaching is too exhausting for me. I apply at Temp Agencies and I learn Microsoft Word, Excel, and PowerPoint. They have these tutorials, so I go to the TempPlace every day until I learn Word, Excel and PowerPoint.

Then I get a job at Intel. It starts out temporary but I then get a permanent position. I am in the Mobile and Handheld Products Group (MHPG.) Everything at Intel has an acronym.

I'm working with wonderful people and meet a nice friend named Sue there. This place is great. And if they could just give a few of their office supplies to schools, the world would be a better place.

I'm still sleeping all weekend. This cannot continue. I am not supposed to be like this. I am going to pare down on my Lithium and continue the Levothyroxine; I'm on Levothyroxine because Lithium messed up my thyroid. I also have to get blood tests every month to see if Lithium's destroying other organs like my liver. It's not this innocuous salt like they make it sound. It's UnderWaterPace and it's swallowing any joy I might have had and I'm done. I am going to gradually pare down on my Lithium. I will never tell my doctor because doctors don't like it when patients think they know their bodies better than the doctors do.

THE COCKTAIL WAITRESS BODY CLOCK

It's been six months, and I've been paring down the Lithium little by little, and I think I'm remembering what I used to be like because I'm getting more like that. I used to enjoy things. I used to not have to sleep all weekend just to do normal life. I still have to sleep all weekend to recover from waking up early five days in a row. I still have this weird body clock that really prefers a cocktails waitress schedule. But I do not prefer a cocktail waitress life. But it's so hard to fight a body clock, and I keep thinking my body will get used to the schedule, but it hasn't yet.

I still don't have much of a life. I think about teaching. It's so much more meaningful than corporate life. I feel like I'm making a difference when I'm teaching. I think that's what I'm supposed to do. But it was so exhausting. I was overcome with Autaustion. I'll keep doing this until it turns Ungood.

* * *

I get laid off.

I guess this means it's time to teach.

TEACH THE CHILDREN AGAIN

I get a job at a public high school called Menlo-Atherton High School and it's a special program for "at-risk" students (I hate that term, but that's what they call it) who are mostly from East Palo Alto. Part of the job is recruiting fifty adult mentors every year – one for each junior in the program.

I used all my savings to live off of when I got laid off and I hope we get paid soon. I don't know if I'll be able to pay rent. And I ran out of my sleep meds. I have to figure out how to get some more, but the insurance hasn't kicked in yet.

* * *

I can't believe this. We have to work for an entire month before we see a dime. I'm not going to be able to pay rent. I'm going to get evicted. *I'm going to be living on the streets again.* I can't do it again. I am going to take care of this. I will tell the principal that this is cruel and unusual punishment and they cannot make people work this hard without getting paid, and I'm going to be evicted.

I write a note to the principal's secretary about my concerns.

DODGED A BULLET

I figure I've dodged a bullet because I sleep all weekend. I vaguely remember getting manic and not being able to sleep, and staying up for two nights in a row and writing weird stuff and listening to all the music I have.

I am called into the principal's office. He shows me a printout of the email I sent to his secretary. Every other word is fuck. What is it about mania that makes my mouth like a truck driver's?

I've only been here a week, and I've ruined my teaching career.

He says, "This smacks of substance abuse. This is not the person I hired."

Well, goddamnit, I've been sober thirteen years now. I can't think of any excuse. I've never told anyone about being crazy. I want to swallow it the minute I hear the words coming out of my mouth:

"I'm bipolar and ran out of medication. I'm so sorry. It won't happen again."

He pulls out his personal checkbook and asks, "Would a loan help?"

I almost replied out of habit, "Oh no, I couldn't," but then I thought, I have to pay the rent, and said, "Well, yes. Thank you so much, and I will repay you the minute I get my first paycheck."

In a flipping month.

But he should have fired me. Turns out someone very close to him is bipolar, so he didn't freak out on the whole issue, because he knows someone. He knows one person. He didn't judge me, and it only took one person.

IMPOSTER TEACHER

I have been stable for about seven years and am still teaching at Menlo-Atherton High School in the Bay Area of Northern California. I love the kids, but I absorb their energy, and they have such hard lives. They live in East Palo Alto and their lives are just chaotic. I come home exhausted, and all I do is create lesson plans, teach, correct papers and sleep. I have no life. And I of course cannot cry, and cannot belly-laugh due to my flattening meds.

I run a Mentor Program for the juniors. It is called Youth Outreach Media Mentor Program (YOMMP.) Youth Outreach Media Mentor Program shows students how to write, storyboard, direct, edit, shoot, and produce shorts, documentaries, and feature films. With mentors' help, students choose a cause they are passionate about, and after the production wraps, they must create action and activism plans which further their cause. I love movies, and so do my students. Movies can open hearts and minds. Running YOMMP while teaching is a lot of hard work, but I think it's making a difference.

I enjoy adolescents so much. They are so honest and funny and creative. The problem is that I have a fundamental problem with authority. When anyone wields power over me, I get enraged. And I don't want to do that to my students. But sometimes they misbehave, and I should (?) wield power over them, but I can't. I don't want to enrage them the way that I get enraged. A teacher shouldn't let students get away with bad behavior, but they have such hard lives, and they are going through so much, and I don't want to contribute to their stress.

So I don't think I'll be able to teach much longer. I've done a good job, in that they appreciate my compassion and tell me they learn a lot from me, but I can't seem to get the hang of being an authority figure. And if I've taught this long and still haven't gotten the hang of it, I don't think it's going to happen.

I've been having insomnia…

HUNTER S. THOMPSON IN MY HEAD

I am walking along the Oakland Pier when I hear HeadHunter and he is talking about how it is weird that we have so much in common. I agree but mention that I have no desire to play with firearms. HeadHunter is my nickname for Hunter S. Thompson when he comes into my head using Johnny Depp's voice. This has been going on since my most recent manic started. It's better than my last manic seventeen years ago because during that one, there were a lot of mumbled voices and it was very confusing but during this one, it's only HeadHunter.

It was almost nine at night, and I'd been wandering the streets of Oakland for about a week. I'd flown to L.A. for various reasons and before that I think I went somewhere else and was wandering. HeadHunter showed up to sort of protect me.

I've been seventeen years sober, sixteen years without a cigarette, take Lithium for manic-depression, and teach English and Computer Applications at Menlo-Atherton High School. Then I just clicked into a manic and couldn't sleep for days and nights on end and that was it. I skipped town.

HeadHunter has encouraged me to go back to drinking and smoking since the past seventeen years have been sort of dour – just too Perfectionistic and serious and depressing. It's much more fun this way. I'm glad he's running the show right now. He's talking to me about how writers should write and what the hell is wrong with me that I'm a writer who doesn't write. I keep telling him I'm as baffled as he is – that all I've ever wanted to do since I wrote Rudolf the Red-Nosed Reindeer when I was five years old was be an author – that authors are my most highly-regarded human-beings - but that I just can't get my ass in gear. But he won't have it. He's really angry about this. He thinks the drinking and smoking will be Hemingwayesque or something and loosen me up to write.

I really hope it works. But the problem when I'm manic is that I'm too scattered to write. When I'm not manic I'm too depressed to write. It's that old dilemma. I don't know how Sylvia Plath ever got anything down. How did that woman do it? I'm not sure how I'm supposed to write this book when I'm on survival mode here – conning people into staying one more night on their credit card at the Executive Inn at the Oakland Pier and last night I was at the Motel Six and then left in the middle of the night when I dozed off and found my shorts around my ankles. I wasn't expecting Nigel to be one of those guys who'd say he'd keep his hands to himself and then break his word. But he was. So I got outta' there.

So I'm not in the position to be hunkering down to write when I'm busy fleeing Motel Sixes in Oakland. I'm disappointed in Nigel.

I think HeadHunter tried to warn me about him but it was in a different voice. I didn't recognize it. Then he started using Johnny Depp's voice like in *Fear and Loathing in Las Vegas* and I recognized him. That's not quite fair, I know. But I've never met Hunter S. Thompson in person, so I think of his voice as Johnny Depp's voice. So when it's in my head, I recognize it that way.

So HeadHunter's mostly a good influence, I think. At least my depression's gone. And he has some very good insight. He's one of my favorite male writers along with Augusten Burroughs. My favorite female writers are too numerous to mention – oh I changed my mind, I have to mention two since I named two males: Sylvia Plath and my writing teacher, Adair Lara.

I see a vintage red Chevrolet convertible parked in front of the Serenade Lounge that looks like the Great Red Shark in Fear and Loathing In Las Vegas. It must be a sign. I'm going into the bar.

"Well, hello, little lady."

"Hi, I'm visiting here from Australia and I don't have any American money. Is there a cover?"

"Well, no. Can I buy you a drink?"

"Oh, sure. Thanks."

HeadHunter's been giving me a hard time about the fact that I'm a writer who doesn't write and maybe it's the fact that I'm sober. So I'm going to start drinking again. All the great writers drink. And I miss smoking too.

Maybe that's why I'm always depressed. Anhedonia. The opposite of hedonism. That's my main problem. I deny myself of all pleasure. I've gotten myself into so much trouble in life doing pleasurable things that I've started living life devoid of all pleasure and this has made for a gray and bland existence.

HeadHunter is trying to help me embrace my hedonism. It's lucky he's entered my life. In fact, I think he's here to save my life.

"Thanks, HeadHunter."

"No problem, sport."

"What did you say, little lady?"

"Oh, I said thanks, I'd like an Irish Coffee."

"Coming right up. What's your name?"

"Diana."

"Nice to meet you."

"What are you doing here all the way from Down Under?"

"I'm a journalist. If you only had one CD to listen to on a desert island – with one outlet and one CD player – what would it be?"

"Interesting question. Let me think about that one for a while. In the meantime, how about this dance? You like Nelly?"

"Sure, but I'm on assignment, so I need to be looking for someone right now. Sorry about that."

"No problem. Nice bag. Where did you get that?"

"Oh, I just got back from the Grammys. Sean Combs gave it to me."

"P. Diddy give you that bag? Let me see that. Ralph Lauren. Look at the chain you got there on that bag. That's some kinda' weapon. You smart to be carryin' that here in Oaktown."

"Yep. While I'm waiting, how about another question. If you had one DVD on that desert island, what would it be?"

"Do the Right Thing."

"That's a great answer. I'm going to write that down. Excuse me, bartender, may I have a napkin?"

"Am I going to be famous now? You gonna' write me up in some kinda' article or do I get to be on the TV or something?"

"We'll just have to see about that. Excuse me, I need to go the lieu." I don't know if they use that British term in Australia, but it just pops out.

"The what?"

"The bathroom."

"I'll watch your purse if you want."

"I'm sure you will."

I had two suitcases being watched by an older couple at the end of the bar. My intuition is impeccable and I kept glancing over there. The suitcases were right under their feet. Bless them.

The bathroom only had one working toilet and there was toilet paper all over the floor. I didn't care. I was a journalist working on a story.

As I was closing the stall door, Hunter S. Thompson came into my head.

"Isn't this better than walking up Santa Cruz Avenue in Menlo Park in the freezing cold?" HeadHunter asks. He is referring to my compulsion to walk when I am manic and my leaving my car at school and wandering off into the streets of Menlo Park, CA.

I had to walk. Whenever I get manic I have to walk. It's imperative. I can't stand and I can't sit. It's like an internal law as necessary as the law of gravity.

HeadHunter continues: "You ditched your car in the D wing of Menlo-Atherton High School. That was insane."

"You do things that make you appear insane all the time."

I retort, "But I'm a famous journalist."

Headhunter counters: "You're a teacher posing as a journalist in a bar in Oakland and you're the only white person in here. I'm a male with firearms and you are a small un-armed female. Just because we're both embarrassed to be Americans in January of 2005 - and that's why you're posing as an Australian - that doesn't mean you can get away with the shit that I can get away with."

I muse, "I thought you were supposed to help me with hedonism. I'm having more fun right now than I've had in years. *Years*. How sad is that? I haven't been allowing myself to have fun. It's been hell. I've been walking around pretending to be happy and yet I'm not. I'm *really* not.

"Then shut the fuck up!"

"Will do."

It's different being on the streets this time but my parents froze my bank account. To protect me. To protect me from myself. I am so mad at them. Yes, I spend a lot of money when I'm manic but that's my business. Now I may as well be a street person wandering around with no money. Did they ever think of that? I guess they figured I'd go back to my apartment with my tail between my legs. No Sir.

JAMES

Since I need to walk, I go outside and wander a bit. I decide that I'd like to be back in San Francisco so I take a bus to get there. It is increasingly difficult to sit still.

I get off the bus and begin to wander.

I see a young man approaching, with a smile on his face. He is wearing a sweatshirt that says "COLLEGE," a pair of baggy jeans, and his skin is the color of redwood tree bark. Gorgeous.

"Hi," he says in a friendly, really low voice.

"Hi," I say.

"My name's James Washington."

"I'm Diana"

"Nice to meet you, Diana."

"You too."

" What'cha doin' out here all by yourself?"

"I'm on my way to Zim's"

"Can I walk you there? I'll protect you."

"Sure."

He has white shoes. I'd better be careful.

"Wanna' hear something cool?" he asks.

"Okay."

"My uncle's Denzel."

"You're lying."

"No – really. We can call him if you want."

"I'd like that. Because I don't believe you."

I light a cigarette.

"You shouldn't smoke."

He lights up a joint.

"Neither should you."

"But this is natural," he quips.

"That's what they all say. Tobacco is natural."

"It's addictive"

"So's that."

"No, it's not."

"It's psychologically addictive."

"I'll give you that."

"It makes you lazy. Cigarettes don't make you lazy." I lecture.

"Let's call him now. I bet there's a pay phone in Zim's," I say

"Sure," he agrees.

We get to Zim's and find a pay phone. James calls a number and is talking and laughing and then mentions that he met the perfect young lady but that she smokes.

"He wants to talk to you."

I get on the phone. It sure sounds like Denzel. The voice on the other end of the line says, "You really shouldn't smoke. You should appreciate James and find something else to occupy your mouth."

"Denzel! Shame on you!"

And he is laughing hysterically.

"I'm just kidding, little lady. Do whatever you like. Just take good care of James. He's a good man."

"Will do."

We get a booth and look at the menu. I decide to get the omelette with mushrooms and spinach and James gets a burger.

"So," he says, "What kind of work do you do?"

"I was in teaching but I got sick and they let me go."

"That's rude."

"I know, right?"

"What kind of sickness did you get?" He asks me.

"I went crazy."

"Crazy how?"

"I had hallucinations, heard voices-"

"What kind of voices?" he interrupts.

"Some of them were scary. Some of them I thought were angels."

"What did they say?"

"They'd tell me who was safe and who was dangerous. They'd tell me when to write and what to write. They'd remind me to eat and sleep – although I couldn't sleep to save my life."

"Sound like real angels to me."

"You never know."

"How long did you go without sleeping?"

"I'm not sure. At least four days. Sometimes more."

"Do you know why it happened?"

"No," I said softly.

We talked about his family, my family, jobs, boyfriends, girlfriends. He told me he'd just gotten out of jail for possession. At three in the morning he was tired. I wasn't tired at all.

"Can I drop you off somewhere?" I asked.

"Well, I'm staying with a friend but I don't have a key. It's too late – or too early – to wake him up."

"You can crash with me tonight. As long as you really were in for possession and you're not an axe murderer."

"I promise I'm not. Thanks so much."

We walk back to the car, but it's locked in the garage. Damn.

"Don't worry about it. My car is just a couple blocks down."

It is about thirteen blocks down and it is really cold.

We decide to play Bob Marley's Legend. Three Little Birds plays as we pull out.

James drives like a maniac but we never get pulled over. He's Hollywood. He's not CIA or FBI. Hollywood is AboveTheFray. They play by their own rules. They don't have to worry about doctors overmedicating them. They self-medicate. Yes, it's dangerous, but they're in control. As long as I'm with James I don't have to worry about cops pulling us over. He has white beads with a white cross hanging from his rear view mirror. Maybe that's why he doesn't get pulled over.

"Is This Love" is playing as we pull into the garage.

Who knows?

"Don't worry, Diana. I'll be a perfect gentleman."

"Thank you, James."

He gets into bed and I lie down next to him.

I can't sleep.

I can't sleep at all.

It's been about three days since I've slept and I figured I'd sleep tonight.

I get up and pace. When I get bored of that I read an old *Vanity Fair* cover to cover. I go outside and smoke a cigarette. Then I read *Time Magazine* cover to cover. I go outside and smoke another cigarette. Then I lie on the couch and try to sleep, but I can't, so I get up and pace some more. I lie back down in bed with James and stare at the ceiling until the sun comes up.

We spend the next two weeks together and it is Heaven. He is so good to me. I am still in the Mind-Skipping place, but when people aren't reacting to me with fear and repulsion, and when I am not alone and fearful, when someone is just accepting of me, the Voices quiet down. He takes good care of me: When I can't sleep he rubs my feet to help me relax, and when I forget to eat, he cooks for me. I am going to marry him.

One night, when we are coming home from the movies, we get pulled over. So much for my theory. The two cops tell James to get out of the car. Then they *slam* him against the car and start roughing him up. I get out and ask what's going on. They tell me it's none of my concern and to get back in the car. They handcuff James and shove him in the squad car. His head bangs against the car. One of them comes over and tells me I will need to drive the car home. I ask again what is going on, and am told, again, that it is none of my concern.

I never see James again.

ALICE'S RESTAURANT

I walk to Village Chevron in Los Altos, CA to pick up my car. I sing Are You Going to San Francisco? (Be Sure to Wear Some Flowers in Your Hair), Get Together, White Rabbit, Revolution, and thought, we need a revolution. WHAT IS GOING ON HERE? I'm not Manic; I'm MAD. Bush is a liar and I COULD DO IT BETTER.

Then I thought, Oh, I must be manic. That was a Delusion of Grandeur. Then I thought, who cares? No, wait, I'm not Manic, I'm MAD. I'm mad at war; it's an anachronism. What are we doing here in 2005 in a war where boys are killing women and children and the Democrats aren't starting a revolution? What is wrong with us?

I'll start it. I'm scrappy.

They'll never see me coming. I'm just a psycho on Kaiser's radar screen - usually misdiagnosed as schizophrenic anyway and given Haldol and Thorazine, shuffling along, getting those pesky side-effects... lockjaw, convulsions. A little inconvenient when you're trying to be a high school teacher.

I'll sue Kaiser and I'll go from there. ("Kaiser... Thrive." HA!) But I'll win. It's so obvious it's 1984 right now in the psychiatric wards with all the cameras everywhere. With the Dogs of War medicating all the artists who might start revolutions. Well, not me. I'm not medicated anymore and I'm MAD. I'm not manic; I'm MAD.

But I have to use the restroom. And I'm walking. And I don't want to get in trouble for public urination. I'm not homeless anymore so I'm stopping at Ranger Kyle's to pee. Ranger Kyle is my friend Sarah's husband;

I met Sarah getting my Teaching Credential and we've been friends ever since. They live in Redwood Grove in Los Altos.

I walk down the driveway off University Ave. in Los Altos and there's day camp going on. I see rich white women in yoga pants and think, are you happy? They look so sad, so harried.

"Hi, I'm Spencer. What's your name?" He has white hair and is about four. *He should be mine. What am I doing in this life?*

"Well hello, Spencer, I'm Diana."

"This is my brother Zachary."

"Hi, Zachary."

"Are you a movie star?"

"No, much better. I'm a teacher."

"Will you be my teacher?"

"I teach high school, so in about ten years, I might be your teacher."

"Will you be my mom?"

"Where's your mom?"

"She left."

"You know that's not your fault, right?"

"I was really bad before she left. She was yelling at me and I said I was sorry but I guess she didn't believe me."

"It's not your fault. Sometimes grown-ups make mistakes. I think she made a mistake."

"Will you be my mommy?"

"Sweetie, I can't be your mommy but I can be your friend. Will you be here tomorrow?"

"Yeah."

"Okay, I'll come visit you tomorrow. Right now I have to use the bathroom." *I'm going to pee in my pants unless I get to the bathroom right now.*

I'm not manic. I'm not homeless. I'm not going in on a 5150. I've relieved myself. I'm free.

"Thanks, Kyle."

"Sure. Sarah's at the doctor and then she's doing errands. I'll have her call you."

"Great. See you later."

Phew. Freedom. No cops. No doctors. I love not being on meds.

I'm finally at Village Chevron.

"Hi."

"Oh, hello, Miss Grippo. All ready for you."

"Thanks, Jay. Want a smoke?"

"Can't smoke now. Working."

"Too bad. How much do I owe you?"

"$324.44."

"Here you go." It always blows me away when I have enough money to pay for things…

And I'm free! Wagons Ho!

I'm going to Cascal, my favorite Mountain View restaurant, for black bean soup. I make twelve calls, including one to SAGE, Students for the Advancement of Global Entrepreneurship.

I stay and smoke and make my calls and there are no cops in sight. Why?

I'm off to Alice's Restaurant because I'm mad at Buck's. I can't believe they wouldn't let me sit there with my laptop and eat soup yesterday. Screw Buck's.

I go in and there are two bikers with Harley Davidson leather jackets on. I love bikers. They're my people. They're evolved.

"What can I get you?"

"I'll take a cup of soup and a Samuel Adams." Drinking is not a moral issue. I have to keep telling myself that because I have seventeen years of sobriety telling me I'm evil for drinking a beer on my summer vacation.

"You got it."

No cops in sight. No MilitaryHaircutMen. No Dogs of War at Alice's Restaurant. I love this place.

I hear an ambulance and get instant diarrhea. They're coming to take me away... oh, no... where the men in white coats...

I hit the restroom and ask two guys to watch my laptop.

"That ain't what we're watchin' right now, honey." Screw you. But I'm going to hold my tongue. I'm not manic...

My favorite show is Stella. I love Michael Ian Black. All my fantasies are unattainable. Oh well. Screw it. I'm scrappy.

At least I didn't tell the guy who was flirting with me to @#$% off like I do when I'm manic. But I'm not manic-depressive. Because there is no such thing. Not manic. Just MAD.

I go to my therapy appointment. This is my fifth one and I'm smarter than she is. She's Kaiser trained so I'll just tell her I did a Thought Record. She worships Thought Records.

Done. Free! Wagon's Ho!

I go to Buck's because I'm trying to be less vengeful. I'm saving all my vengeance for Kaiser.

"Hi, sweetie. You want a Sam Adams?"

"Yep. And some French Onion soup."

Good. Patricia's here. I'm a huge tipper so she likes me. Money talks. I'll never understand why people aren't good tippers. It's so worthwhile to make a waitress' day. I remember when I worked at Chevy's in Larkspur when I was getting my teaching credential and one huge tip could totally make my day. It's so fun to do that. It's like paying someone's toll. I did that when I went to the writer's class in Sonoma on Sat. and it's so fun.

I have to pee of course but I'm in a restaurant and I'm not homeless and I have money to pay so there's no problem.

"Excuse me, would you mind watching that laptop while I use the restroom?"

"You bet. We'll watch it closely. The restrooms are right around the corner, darlin."

"Thanks." Bikers. I love bikers.

I use the restroom and there's no paranoia. It's a beautiful thing. I'm not going to be kicked out of here. I'm not going to be taken away by the cops and off to Hotel California. I'm free. Wagons Ho. All it takes is cash. Have cash, will travel.

I walk back and BikerDudes ask me if I want to eat my French Onion Soup at the bar next to them since I wouldn't want to mess up my laptop. They have a point. Why not. They're evolved. They're bikers.

"Sure, why not?"

"So, what's your name?"

"Diana." No Australian tourist lines. No conning. Just tell the truth. Not manic.

"Nice to meet you, Diana. I'm Ken. This here's Tom."

"Nice to meet you both."

"So whatcha' workin' on?"

"Fear and Loathing in Los Altos."

"Oh man, I once had to babysit Hunter S. Thompson when he was in Wyoming and it was terrible."

"What was terrible?"

"He kept getting in trouble everywhere we went. I had to clean up all his messes. He had me stop on the way to the hotel for a bottle of Jack

Daniels and he finished it before we got to the hotel. It shattered my image. I'd read everything he'd ever written and I was so disappointed."

"Nobody said he was balanced. Give him a break." He is criticizing my God. I LOVE HST's writing and I will not have this guy badmouthing Hunter S. Thompson, for Christ's sake.

"Nah, man, it bummed me out."

"Kicked him right off that pedestal, huh? It's not his fault you had him on a pedestal. Nobody belongs on a pedestal," I observe.

"He was on mine though, and that weekend just bummed me out, man. So what's the book about?"

"Bag lady."

"Shopping cart?"

"Yep."

"Oh, if you want to see some bag ladies go the Tenderloin. Ever been there?" Uh. YEAH. Lived there for two years. *Shhh... Don't tell.*

"I go to Glide Memorial, so yeah, I'm familiar with it."

"You oughtta' check out San Jose near the Guadalupe River. My friend's a cop and we had to help clear out these pipes and there were all these bums living in them."

"That's rough."

"Hey, you wanna' come with us to A Trattoria? It's in Redwood City. You can follow us."

"Sure. Let me pay for my French Onion soup first." Money. I love money. When I have money I don't get sent to jail. Or Hotel California. It's such a direct correlation. I need more money. I can't spend any money for two weeks since I only get paid once a month and my budget was worked out perfectly until MilitaryHaircutMan messed with my car.

We drive to the restaurant. They're both on Harleys and I feel safe. The cops won't mess with me if I have two bikers on my side. They're evolved. I need to remember to install some anti-SpyWare software on my computer before I email my diary entry for the day to Adair. The number 33 pops into my head – must be the number of files infected by SpyWare. So good to be Sam again. When I get psychic hits I pretend I'm Sam from Bewitched the way I used to do when I was little.

"Hey, darlin', what are you working on there?"

I usually get my psychic hits when I'm drawing so I'd pulled out the Alice's Motorcycle Shop logo I'm working on.

"It's a logo. Can I borrow your jacket so I can draw the Harley wings?"

"You bet, but I have a better patch on my vest. It's a skull smokin' a cigar and there's a poker hand and some booze. You gotta' check it out."

"Where's your vest?"

"Home. You should go to this place in San Jose off Capitol Expressway called Just Leather and they have really big ones. I could only fit a little one on my vest. Ken, I got Tiny to get the big one. Darlin', you gotta' meet Tiny."

"Is he a big Samoan guy or something?"

"You know him?"

"Most people named Tiny are big. It was just a guess."

"I like the way you've done the lettering like the old Filmore posters. That's hot. You oughtta' check out the movie *Alice's Restaurant* with Arlo Guthrie. His dad was dyin' – oh, I'm not gonna' tell you anymore. You gotta' check it out."

"Will do. Do you think I should have a black or white background?"

"It looks good how you have it. Don't wreck it."

"Okay." Easier for me. I don't feel like coloring the whole background black anyway. I need to check my voicemail.

"Excuse me while I check my voicemail." I pull out a cigarette.

"Oh, you just wanna' have a smoke."

"Yeah, got that right. I'm addicted."

"You really should quit. Bad for you."

"I'm in a hedonistic stage right now so I'm going to keep doing it."

"Stuff'll kill ya." We're all going to die; I'd rather enjoy myself while I'm here.

"Listen, do you go up to fat people and tell them to stop eating so much?"

"Sometimes."

"Well, don't. And let me smoke. I'm going over there so I won't blow it in your face. Live and Let Live."

"That's cool. Whatever."

I listen to my voicemail.

"Hello, Diana, this is Lindy and you've won a free evaluation at our modeling agency. I'm bringing in my national director so if you can come Thursday the 21st at 11am that would be great. Give me a call back at 415-xxx-xxxx."

I don't want to be a model. I want to be a talk-show host and bring in the homeless and the Vets and the rape victims. They're all the ones in the psych wards. And it's WAR. It's war that fills up the psych wards.

I'm ready to leave and go write my diary entry for the day.

"I'm going to head out. Thanks for dinner!"

"Hey, where ya' goin', Blondie? Dude, she reminds me of Blondie."

"Gotta' get up early."

"Alright, darlin', we'll see you later. But if you change your mind we'll be at the Pioneer Inn."

"Okay. Later!"

"Drive safe."

"Will do." Bless bikers. Free dinner. I have no money. And I got free dinner. Woo-hoo!

I go home and see that Bob Woodward and Carl Bernstein are on my boyfriend's show. But Jon Stewart seems happily married so I'll need to cross him off my list at some point. Jim Carrey's still single I think. But how would I ever meet Jim Carrey? Well, I did almost meet him when I went to his and Andy Kaufman's talk in L.A. about *Eternal Sunshine of the Spotless Mind*. I love that movie. I have such a crush on Jim Carrey. Everyone was bothering him, shaking his hand and he was so gracious so even though I want to marry him, I didn't introduce myself. He was so polite to everyone and I just didn't want to be one more bothersome fan. I love Jim Carrey. He's my dream man.

I've got to set more attainable goals.

Bob Woodward talks about the press and how they need to be more aggressive. Well, I'm not the press but I'm happy to be aggressive. Because Bush just makes me so scared. I get nauseous every time I hear him speak his FraternitySpeak and his PowerFake.

I watch Reno 911 which I LOVE. Man, I love that show. Then finally, Stella comes on. Another unattainable goal: Michael Ian Black. Yum. There's a commercial for Stopsign software and I install it. 33 files infected. Bingo. I'm free. No more SpyWare. I'm free! Wagon's Ho!

THE BEST LUCK

I had to go to the hospital again. I'm out now. After my slip, I decide to go to A.A. instead of doing it myself. I meet so many nice people and I love The Twelve Steps. I will list them later, but some of my favorites are steps 3, 8 and 11.

Step 3 is "Made a decision to turn our will and our lives over to the care of God <u>as we understood Him</u>." Turning my will and my life over to the care of God as I understand Him affects my intuition and decisions in positive ways.

Step 8 is "Made a list of all persons we have harmed, and became willing to make amends to them all." This is very important, especially since mania leaves such destruction in my wake.

Step 11 is "Sought through prayer and meditation to improve our conscious contact with God <u>as we understand Him</u>, praying only for knowledge of His will for us and the power to carry that out." If I listen to my Inner Voice, it will usually tell me what the right thing to do is.

So I'm feeling a bit better, but I'm confronted with the fact that I have no job, and it is October, so all the teaching jobs are accounted for and I'll have to wait until next year to get another teaching job.

I decide to just get some job – any job – to pay the bills. So I work at Chico's and here is a typical scenario: I spend two hours with a woman, picking out outfits for her, chatting her up, running back and forth to fetch different sizes, and my colleague swoops in at the very end with a scarf. She rings up the sale and gets the commission. Who does that? She has a rich husband and is just doing this as a sort of hobby. Why be that way?

When I get my first paycheck, I go to the Apple store to buy my first iPhone. I get it all set up, look around, and think, I want to work *here*. This is where I should be.

It takes awhile, but I get the job, and it is the best luck I have had in years. Everything changes.

THANK YOU, APPLE

I work at Apple now. I was in the top five in sales for five years and have been number one or number two in sales for the past three years. I should do better at selling Apple Care though. I am always working on that. I encircle myself in white light every morning to keep my energy up. When I taught high school, I absorbed everybody's energy, so that by the time I got home, my energy was completely depleted. I had no life. As mentioned, all I did was teach school, prepare lesson plans, correct papers, and sleep. I feel much better now.

It may seem weird to encircle myself in the white light of God's love and Divine power, but it works for me. I've also been reading a lot about channeling and listening to channeled material like Abraham channeled by Esther Hicks. It makes a lot of sense. The idea is that this is not all there is. Of course not. Any religion can tell you that. It's just that channeled material is more accessible to me than religion. Instead of an all-powerful God up in the sky somewhere, Abraham talks about our Inner Being and how it's a part of Source, and how it's eternal.

Here is a synopsis of Abraham-Hicks' teachings:

"You are a physical extension of that which is non-physical.

"You are here in this body because you chose to be here.

"The basis of your life is freedom; the purpose of your life is joy.

"You are a creator. You create with your every thought.

"Anything that you can imagine is yours to be or do or have.

"As you are choosing your thoughts, your emotions are guiding you.

"The Universe adores you for it knows your broadest intentions.

"Relax into your well-being. All is well. (Really it is!)

"You are a creator of thoughtways on your unique path of joy.

"Actions to be taken and possessions to be exchanged are by-products of your focus on joy.

"You may appropriately depart your body without illness or pain.

"You can not die; you are everlasting life.

"P.S. It is not necessary for even one other person to understand the Laws of the Universe or the processes that we are offering here in order for you to have a wonderful, happy, productive Life Experience – for you are the attractor of your experience. Just you!"

Abraham goes on "Rampages of Appreciation" through Esther, and they are great.

I also like the channeled entity Michael. They talk about Soul Age, how we come in with different roles, and how the number of lifetimes we've had affects how we see the world.

I pray all the time.

I pull a Tarot Card every morning before I go to work to see what I should be on the lookout for. This morning it was The Star: "Stars represent hopes and wishes. They don't promise results now; rather, they are about having faith that a situation will work out and be well sometime in the future."

I've been stable for five years now. I had a manic episode five years ago, and Apple let me go on a paid leave while I was in the hospital. I love Apple. They've been so good to me. Everyone's nice and supportive. All the way up to Tim Cook. I've met him several times and he's truly kind. He is really supportive and positive, and a great listener.

THE WONDERS OF MODERN MEDICATION

I tend to have an episode during election season. I've always followed politics closely and have remained hopeful that our elected officials are moral, ethical and have the American people's best interests at heart. When it's looking like we're going in the wrong direction, I tend to have an episode. This can't be a coincidence.

If you suffer from some sort of mood disorder, you may want to look not only at what's going on in your personal life, but also at what's going on in the political landscape. Part of having an episode, I believe, is a Spiritual Emergency. Some sort of spiritual path can really help.

I am not here to tell you to take medication or not to take medication. If you believe you need medication, take it. It can do wonders. I take Abilify now and it is working well for me. I prefer it to Lithium, which "flattened" me and kept me in a state of depression. People who are bipolar are discouraged from taking anti-depressants because they can induce a manic episode. There is also a compromise: You can get a prescription for a mood stabilizer, and when you feel you are slipping into an episode, you can take it. Lithium might work for you, and there are other mood stabilizers that you can try.

I have revised my theory about Kaiser: It is not evil; it is good. After the hospital I went to a residential program for a week and it was a really good program. It was encouraged by and covered by Kaiser, and it taught Dialectical Behavior Therapy.

Come to think of it, I have also revised my theory about medication. Some people just need medication. Taking Abilify has improved my mood, so it's a matter of finding the one that works for you.

Just don't discount your Spiritual Emergency. We need to take care of our Souls. Search for a spiritual path; it can make all the difference. You must also do some work: Therapy and Dialectical Behavior Therapy are very important elements to mental health. It is not just about taking a pill and going on our way.

A SPIRITUAL FOUNDATION

To feel better, I have found that music works wonders. It can lift us up. It can make us happy. It can solidify our love. It can give us hope. And it can give us courage.

But alas, music alone is not enough.

We only need look at the number of artists who have self-destructed.

We need a foundation. A spiritual foundation. A spiritual path that has worked for me is the Twelve Steps. I use it for depression. I am bipolar so I have highs and lows. During my highs, I have delusions, hallucinations, stay awake for four days and nights, forget to eat and drink, and spend and give away all my money. The upside is that I've had some incredible spiritual experiences.

During my lows, I lose my spiritual connection. That is why I started working the Twelve Steps for the depression. I have tweaked them below to work for depression, and I'll probably get in troubled with someone, but… whatever. I mean, hey, why should addicts be the only ones who get to work the Steps?

Some people may have trouble with the word "God," but it is very clear that it is a God "as you understand Him." It can be any Deity from any religion, or it can be the Universe, or Source – anything that works for you!

So here they are:

The Twelve Steps:

1. "We admitted we were powerless over depression – that our lives had become unmanageable."

2. "Came to believe that a Power greater than ourselves could restore us to sanity."
3. "Made a decision to turn our will and our lives over to the care of God <u>as we understood Him.</u>"
4. "Made a searching and fearless moral inventory of ourselves."
5. "Admitted to God, to ourselves, and to another human being the exact nature of our wrongs."
6. "Were entirely ready to have God remove all these defects of character."
7. "Humbly asked Him to remove our shortcomings."
8. "Made a list of all persons we had harmed, and became willing to make amends to them all."
9. "Made direct amends to such people wherever possible, except when to do so would injure them or others."
10. "Continued to take personal inventory and when we were wrong promptly admitted it."
11. "Sought through prayer and meditation to improve our conscious contact with God <u>as we understood Him</u>, praying only the knowledge of His will for us and the power to carry that out."
12. "Having had a spiritual awakening as a result of these steps, we tried to carry this message to others who are suffering, and to practice these principles in all our affairs."

I encourage you to get a copy of the Big Book of Alcoholics Anonymous to read examples of how these steps may be carried out. Though you may not have substance abuse problems, the solution is a spiritual one and will work on depression as well as substance abuse.

DIALECTICAL BEHAVIOR THERAPY

Besides a spiritual path, I've found Dialectical Behavior Therapy very helpful. Dialectical Behavior Therapy (DBT) was developed by Marsha M. Linehan and provides tools to help with two opposing concepts: Accepting what is, and embracing change. It helps identify triggers and assess which coping skills to use to avoid undesired reactions.

DBT uses mindful awareness largely derived from meditative practice to help with emotional regulation, distress tolerance and reality-testing.

Besides using mindful awareness, the skills stress behavioral changes, such as opposite action, to help alleviate stress. Watching comedy when you are feeling depressed is an example of this. As mentioned earlier, exercising when you feel like lying in bed and reaching out when you feel like isolating are examples of opposite action. Again, it is very difficult to think your way out of a depression, but sometimes your can *act* your way out of a depression.

One aspect of Dialectical Behavior Therapy I find incredibly helpful is the concept of Radical Acceptance. This is an excerpt from the magazine Psychology Today written by Cecilia Dintino:

"Radical Acceptance means complete and total openness to the facts of reality as they are. There are three reasons why:

"Denying reality does nothing to change reality.

"All change begins with acceptance.

"Pain cannot be avoided. It is just a part of life, and we are built to tolerate it. When you don't accept pain, it turns into agony. Pain + Non-acceptance = Suffering

"To radically accept means you do it all the way – with your full body, mind, and spirit. It is not a one-time fix. It is a practice.

"You have to stop pounding the wall. Instead, gently lean your body against it and slowly let yourself slide down to the ground, soften your face, gentle your breath, turn the palms of your hands open, and just for this moment, accept what it.

"And then do it again.

"Radical acceptance is the way out of hell."

There are many useful skills in DBT and I encourage you to go to Amazon and purchase one of Marsha Linehan's books, as I am not licensed to provide all the details of the therapy.

Trust me: It is really helpful!

CALLING ALL ANGELS

I am cleaning out a drawer and find a small notebook where I've entitled an entry "Calling All Angels." I fill up many notebooks when I'm manic. I rarely reference the source of the material. As it turns out, it is from a calendar I have called Messages from Your Angels Perpetual Flip Calendar by Doreen Virtue. This is what my entry says:

"Working in conjunction with Heavenly guides, your changes will come about in a monumental way.

"As you make your changes, they will go as quickly as you feel comfortable.

"Should you desire an instant change, that is certainly available to you, as your heart desires.

"See the inner joy within everyone, regardless of the surface conditions that appear.

"As you see the holiness within others, you more readily see this Divinity within your own self.

"Know that you are God's lovely child!

"With trust, the rest falls easily into place.

"Begin sharing with your partner the contents of your heart: your dreams and desires.

"Be very honest with yourself about all the aspects of this situation that you are considering.

"Concentrate on giving service in a way that brings you great pleasure and enjoyment. Make your only focus be, 'How may I serve?' and everything will be given unto you.

"Do not delay in giving service by awaiting the day when you leave your present job, for many opportunities to give joyfully await you now.

"Your soul will keep you safe and give you the clear and loving guidance you seek.

"Be not afraid of your own greatness, but allow us to mirror it for you during our communications.

"As you witness out greatness visually, and with naked ears fully opened to love's voice, there you will witness your own Divinity.

"An emotional or physical block is not a reality unless you focus upon it in a constant state of awareness.

"Each relationship has, at its heart, a holy purpose.

"We angels could never cease to love you, not now or ever.

"Uplift the people in your life by surrounding them in an aura of the whitest light.

"Know that your loved ones are being taken care of – whether they are in the physical plane or among us in the spirit world.

"We shall not let go of your loved ones, nor of you.

"No matter what physical actions a human may make, our love goes on without condition or judgment.

"Be gentle with yourselves, Dearest Ones, and know that you live close to God's heart.

"You, who have such power that it is unequaled by any other, could no more be powerless than could God.

"We, who are assigned to watch over your care, cover directly from the same Great Mind that is within each one of you.

"The bliss of the Creator forever permeates all of creation, and it is only in the forgetting that misery exists.

"You are already in the midst of God's blissful reality, and you need not seek it a moment longer.

"We help you to remember your divine nature, to be loving and kind, to discover and polish your talents for the betterment of the world, and to keep yourself from harm's way before your time.

"We are with you to enact God's plan of peace.

"We angels help you be more peaceful, because one person at a time, a world of peaceful people equals a peaceful world.

"You aren't wasting our time if you ask for "small" favors. After all, there are unlimited numbers of us, with unlimited amounts of time.

"While it is true that challenges do make you grow, peace leads to even bigger growth spurts.

"By being a reflection of peacefulness, you are a shining example of God's love.

"We, your guardian angels, are personally assigned to you for your entire life. You are never alone.

"Each of you – regardless of faith, character, or lifestyle – has at least two guardian angels. Whether you choose to listen to us though, is an entirely different matter.

"Everyone has an equal ability to communicate with us, because everyone is equally 'gifted' spiritually.

"The more you can relax, the more easily you will be able to consciously commune with us.

"Children do not care whether they are imagining their angel visions; they simply enjoy and accept them. As a result, little ones easily see and hear us, their guardian angels.

"Allow no fear to 'interfear' with your domain of happiness, for that is God's Kingdom of great blessings.

"You are more powerful than any fearful force. Your Divine willingness can out-will any darkness that the world has ever seen.

"True angelic experiences feel warm, safe, loving, and comfortable.

"We speak to your in response to your queries. So, you can kick-start a conversation simply by directing a question to us.

"Is there a question that you have, or some area of your life in which you desire guidance? Take a moment right now and mentally ask us your question.

"Even if you cannot hear us answering you right now, be assured that we can definitely hear you!

"We orbit around you much like you see the stars in the sky hovering around nearby planets.

"No matter what, you can always count on our unconditional and continuous love.

"Finding a feather, a coin, a stopped clock, moved objects in your home, lights flickering, the television set turning off or on independently, or other visual oddities, lets you know that one of us is saying, "Hello, I am here."

"Seeing a mental movie that provides you with true information about a person or situation, or that gives you guidance about your life purpose or making changes, is a sign of being in our presence."

I read this entry often and it gives me hope. I am not sure why I've had these experiences, but I do know that spirituality has saved me from the rollercoaster in my mind. I have a wonderful life ahead of me, and I release any negativity that is behind me. I am hoping that music, spirituality, Dialectical Behavior Therapy, and (if necessary) medication, can help others chart their course.

MUSIC IS THE LANGUAGE OF THE SOUL

"Music Is the Language Of the Soul": This was embroidered onto a picture, along with some musical instruments, that my grandmother gave me when I was little. I played the piano, flute, and violin. But what I love most is to sing. There is nothing better than to memorize a melody, to memorize the lyrics, and to know them forever.

You can sing songs to yourself, sing songs in the shower, or belt them out in the car. It totally changes your mood. I feel bad for people who grow up with music without melodies. I think we need to bring them back.

So I compiled a list of songs that make me feel good. They will make you feel good too. They will make you smile. They will make you think.

I have marked reggae music with an asterisk, as reggae artists have a spiritual foundation. That is why I encourage people of all races to listen to reggae music. Reggae artists have this spiritual foundation. That is why we do not witness them self-destructing.

I have marked the songs dealing with Social Justice with two asterisks.

When people ask me what my favorite song is, I cannot answer them. Because I have 2,100 of them. And here they are…

THE LIST:

1. Rolling In the Deep: Adele
2. Hello: Adele & 2Pac
3. Sweet Emotion: Aerosmith
4. Dream On: Aerosmith
5. Remember: Aerosmith
6. Kings and Queens: Aerosmith
7. Lost In Love: Air Supply
8. Down In A Hole: Alice In Chains
9. Would? : Alice In Chains
10. Man In A Box: Alice In Chains
11. Fallin': Alicia Keyes
12. If I Ain't Got You: Alicia Keyes
13. No One: Alicia Keyes
14. Gramercy Park: Alicia Keyes
15. Girl On Fire: Alicia Keyes
16. A Woman's Worth: Alicia Keyes
17. Karma: Alicia Keyes
18. You Don't Know My Name: Alicia Keyes
19. Underdog: Alicia Keyes
20. Unbreakable: Alicia Keyes
21. Superwoman: Alicia Keyes
22. Love Is Blind: Alicia Keyes
23. Blue Sky: The Allman Brothers Band

24. Crazy Love: The Allman Brothers Band
25. Whipping Post: The Allman Brothers Band
26. Ramblin' Man: The Allman Brothers Band
27. Melissa: The Allman Brothers Band
28. Midnight Rider: The Allman Brothers Band
29. You're the Only Woman: Ambrosia
30. Daisy Jane: America
31. Ventura Highway: America
32. I Need You: America
33. Lonely People: America
34. Rehab: Amy Winehouse
35. Dark Road: Annie Lennox
36. Walking On Broken Glass: Annie Lennox
37. Little Bird: Annie Lennox
38. Waiting In Vain: Annie Lennox & Steven Lipson
39. Into the West: Annie Lennox
40. A Thousand Beautiful Things: Annie Lennox
41. Don't Let It Bring You Down: Annie Lennox & Steven Lipson
42. I Say A Little Prayer: Aretha Franklin
43. Respect: Aretha Franklin
44. Hold Your Head Up: Argent
45. Summer of Love: B-52's
46. Revolution Earth: B-52's
47. Dreamland: B-52's
48. Debbie: B-52's
49. Loveshack B-52's
50. Seagull: Bad Company
51. Shooting Star: Bad Company
52. Ready for Love: Bad Company

53. Feel Like Makin' Love: Bad Company
54. Live For the Music: Bad Company
55. Can't Get Enough: Bad Company
56. Silver, Blue and Gold: Bad Company
57. Love Me Somebody: Bad Company
58. When I See You Smile: Bad English
59. Looks Like We Made It: Barry Manilow
60. Weekend In New England: Barry Manilow
61. Wouldn't It Be Nice: Beach Boys
62. Good Vibrations: Beach Boys
63. Here Comes the Sun: Beatles
64. Help!: Beatles
65. Eleanor Rigby: Beatles
66. Something: Beatles
67. I Wanna' Hold Your Hand: Beatles
68. Yesterday: Beatles
69. Ob-La-Di, Ob-La-Da: Beatles
70. We Can Work It Out: Beatles
71. Let It Be: Beatles
72. Hey Jude: Beatles
73. Revolution: Beatles * *
74. All You Need Is Love: Beatles
75. The Fool On the Hill: Beatles
76. A Day In the Life: Beatles
77. More Than A Woman: Bee Gees
78. Tragedy: Bee Gees
79. Too Much Heaven: Bee Gees
80. Heaven Is A Place On Earth: Belinda Carlisle
81. Beautiful People: Benny Benassi and Chris Brown

82. Masquerade: Berlin
83. The Metro: Berlin
84. The Rose: Bette Midler
85. From A Distance: Bette Midler
86. Naughty Girl: Beyoncé
87. Crazy In Love: Beyoncé (feat. Jay-Z)
88. Black Parade: Beyoncé
89. Freedom (feat. Kendrick Lamar) : Beyoncé
90. Love On Top: Beyoncé
91. Lovely Day: Bill Withers
92. Ain't No Sunshine: Bill Withers
93. Highway Song: Blackfoot
94. Where Is the Love? : Black Eyed Peas
95. I Gotta Feeling: Black Eyed Peas
96. Let's Get It Started: Black Eyed Peas
97. FEEL THE BEAT: Black Eyed Peas
98. My Humps: Black Eyed Peas
99. RITMO (Bad Boys For Life) : Black Eyed Peas & J Balvin
100. Just Can't Get Enough: Black Eyed Peas
101. Call Me: Blondie
102. Rapture: Blondie
103. God Bless the Child: Blood, Sweat & Tears
104. Spinning Wheel: Blood, Sweat & Tears
105. And When I Die: Blood, Sweat & Tears
106. You've Made Me So Very Happy: Blood, Sweat & Tears
107. Exodus: Bob Marley & The Wailers * *
108. Waiting In Vain: Bob Marley & The Wailers *
109. Three Little Birds: Bob Marley & The Wailers *
110. Get Up, Stand Up: Bob Marley & The Wailers * *

111. Is This Love: Bob Marley & The Wailers *
112. Stir It Up: Bob Marley & The Wailers *
113. So Much Trouble In the World: Bob Marley & The Wailers * *
114. Positive Vibration: Bob Marley & The Wailers *
115. Beautiful Loser: Bob Segar and the Silver Bullet Band
116. Turn the Page: Bob Segar and the Silver Bullet Band
117. Night Moves: Bob Segar and the Silver Bullet Band
118. Hollywood Nights: Bob Segar and the Silver Bullet Band
119. Runaway: Bon Jovi
120. Livin' On A Prayer: Bon Jovi
121. Wanted Dead Or Alive: Bon Jovi
122. More Than A Feeling: Boston
123. Peace of Mind: Boston
124. Long Time: Boston
125. Rock and Roll Band: Boston
126. Long Time: Boston
127. Hitch A Ride: Boston
128. Something About You: Boston
129. Let Me Take You Home Tonight: Boston
130. Don't Look Back: Boston
131. Feelin' Satisfied: Boston
132. Amanda: Boston
133. Cool the Engines: Boston
134. I Want Candy: Bow Wow Wow
135. Lido Shuffle: Boz Scaggs
136. Strawberry Letter 23: The Brothers Johnson
137. Stomp! : The Brothers Johnson
138. The Way It Is: Bruce Hornsby and the Range
139. Thunder Road: Bruce Springsteen

140. Born to Run: Bruce Springsteen
141. Just the Way You Are: Bruno Mars
142. Marry You: Bruno Mars
143. Locked Out of Heaven: Bruno Mars
144. When I Was Your Man: Bruno Mars
145. Summer of '69: Bryan Adams
146. Run to You: Bryan Adams
147. Don't Stop the Dance: Bryan Ferry
148. More Than This: Bryan Ferry
149. Avalon: Bryan Ferry and Roxy Music
150. Expecting to Fly: Buffalo Springfield
151. For What It's Worth (There's Something Happenin' Here): Buffalo Springfield * *
152. I Am A Child: Buffalo Springfield
153. Questions: Buffalo Springfield
154. Mr. Tambourine Man: The Byrds
155. Eight Miles High: The Byrds
156. Turn! Turn! Turn! : The Byrds * *
157. So You Want to Be A Rock 'N Roll Star: The Byrds
158. Jesus Is Just Alright: The Byrds
159. Gonna' Make You Sweat: C & C Music Factory
160. The Right Thing to Do: Carly Simon
161. Anticipation: Carly Simon
162. Haven't Got Time for the Pain: Carly Simon
163. Sweet Seasons: Carole King
164. Brother, Brother: Carole King
165. Only Love Is Real: Carole King
166. Nightingale: Carole King
167. Believe In Humanity: Carole King
168. Jazzman: Carole King

169. Superstar: The Carpenters
170. Top of the World: The Carpenters
171. Close to You: The Carpenters
172. Yesterday: The Carpenters
173. Bless the Beasts and Children: The Carpenters
174. It's Going to Take Some Time: The Carpenters
175. It's All I Can Do: The Cars
176. Good Times Roll: The Cars
177. Just What I Needed: The Cars
178. You're All I've Got Tonight: The Cars
179. Moving In Stereo: The Cars
180. All Mixed Up: The Cars
181. Peace Train: Cat Stevens * *
182. Beginnings: Chicago
183. Call On Me: Chicago
184. Make Me Smile: Chicago
185. I've Been Searchin' So Long: Chicago
186. Saturday In the Park: Chicago
187. Dialogue Parts I & II: Chicago
188. Does Anybody Really Know What Time It Is: Chicago
189. Colour My World: Chicago
190. Just You 'N Me: Chicago
191. Feelin' Stronger Every Day: Chicago
192. Make Me Smile: Chicago
193. Red: Chris Brown
194. Troubled Waters: Chris Brown
195. Dear God: Chris Brown
196. Wicked Game: Chris Isaak
197. Beautiful: Christina Aguilera

198. Arthur's Theme: Christopher Cross
199. Sailing: Christopher Cross
200. Under the Milky Way: The Church
201. Source Of Energy: Clear Conscience *
202. Give Thanks: Clear Conscience (feat. 77 Jefferson & Jack Mufasa) *
203. There's A Fire: Clear Conscience (feat. Benton) *
204. No Worries: Clear Conscience (feat. Benton) *
205. Everything & More: Clear Conscience *
206. Broken Glass: Clear Conscience *
207. Long Time: Clear Conscience (feat. Toko Tasi & Doug Means) *
208. Precious and Few: Climax
209. Adventure of a Lifetime: Coldplay
210. Clocks: Coldplay
211. Hymn for the Weekend: Coldplay (feat. Beyoncé)
212. Dancing: Cole Knox & Raph Ryuichi
213. New Religion: Cole Knox & Raph Ryuichi
214. Top Down: Cole Knox & Raph Ryuichi
215. Artificially Happy: Cole Knox & Raph Ryuichi
216. Easy: The Commodores
217. Mmm Mmm Mmm Mmm: Crash Test Dummies
218. Sunshine of Your Love: Cream
219. Crossroads: Cream
220. I Feel Free: Cream
221. Suite: Judy Blue Eyes: Crosby, Stills & Nash
222. Long Time Gone: Crosby, Stills & Nash * *
223. Shadow Captain: Crosby, Stills & Nash
224. Cathedral: Crosby, Stills & Nash
225. Just A Song Before I Go: Crosby, Stills & Nash
226. Cary On: Crosby, Stills, Nash & Young

227. Questions: Crosby, Stills & Nash
228. Southern Cross: Crosby, Stills & Nash
229. Love the One You're With: Crosby, Stills & Nash
230. Teach Your Children: Crosby, Stills & Nash
231. Woodstock: Crosby, Stills & Nash
232. Wooden Ships: Crosby, Stills & Nash
233. Our House: Crosby, Stills & Nash
234. 49 Bye-Byes: Crosby, Stills & Nash
235. Ohio: Crosby, Stills & Nash * *
236. Country Girl: Crosby, Stills & Nash
237. Don't Dream It's Over: Crowded House
238. Lovesong: The Cure
239. Just Like Heaven: The Cure
240. The Lovecats: The Cure
241. Friday I'm In Love: The Cure
242. Why Can't I Be You? : The Cure
243. Time After Time: Cyndi Lauper
244. Get Lucky (feat. Pharrell Williams) : Daft Punk
245. Part of the Plan: Dan Fogelberg
246. To the Morning: Dan Fogelberg
247. There's A Place in the World for a Gambler: Dan Fogelberg
248. Run for the Roses: Dan Fogelberg
249. Power Of Gold: Dan Fogelberg
250. As the Raven Flies: Dan Fogelberg
251. Sara Smile: Daryl Hall & John Oates
252. So High (Rock Me Baby and Roll Me Away) : Dave Mason
253. To the Last Whale: David Crosby & Graham Nash * *
254. Babylon: David Gray
255. Titanium: David Guetta (feat. Sia)

256. When Love Takes Over: David Guetta
257. Lovers On the Sun: David Guetta
258. Turn Me On: David Guetta
259. Battle: David Guetta
260. Just Like Paradise: David Lee Roth
261. You Spin Me 'Round: Dead Or Alive
262. Soul Meets Body: Death Cab for Cutie
263. Groove Is In the Heart: Deee Lite
264. Highway Star: Deep Purple
265. Woman from Tokyo: Deep Purple
266. Smoke On the Water: Deep Purple
267. Armageddon It: Def Leppard
268. Photograph: Def Leppard
269. Love Bites: Def Leppard
270. Rock of Ages: Def Leppard
271. Hysteria: Def Leppard
272. Warrior: Demi Lovato
273. Personal Jesus: Depeche Mode
274. Just Can't Get Enough: Depeche Mode
275. Enjoy the Silence: Depeche Mode
276. Strangelove: Depeche Mode
277. People Are People: Depeche Mode
278. Policy Of Truth: Depeche Mode
279. Layla: Derek & the Dominos
280. Independent Woman Part I: Destiny's Child
281. Survivor: Destiny's Child
282. Om Namah Shivayah: Deva Primal
283. Whip It: Devo
284. Upside Down: Diana Ross

285. Love Hangover: Diana Ross
286. Here With Me: Dido
287. Holy Diver: Dio
288. Rainbow In the Dark: Dio
289. The Last In Line: Dio
290. Man On the Silver Mountain: Dio
291. Walk On By: Dionne Warwick
292. Then Came You: Dionne Warwick
293. Dance With Me: Diplo, Thomas Red & Young Thug
294. Get It Right: Diplo (feat. MO)
295. Money for Nothing: Dire Straits
296. Latch: Disclosure (feat. Sam Smith)
297. Cake by the Ocean: DNCE
298. Drift Away: Dobie Gray
299. Islands In the Stream: Dolly Parton & Kenny Rogers
300. Take Her Place: Don Diablo (feat. ARIZONA)
301. The Boys of Summer: Don Henley
302. The End of the Innocence: Don Henley
303. Not Enough Love In the World: Don Henley
304. Sunset Grill: Don Henley
305. I Will Not Go Quietly: Don Henley
306. Dirty Laundry: Don Henley
307. Vincent: Don Mclean
308. American Pie: Don Mclean
309. And I Love You So: Don Mclean
310. I Feel Love: Donna Summer
311. Love To Love You Baby: Donna Summer
312. A Song For You: Donny Hathaway *
313. The Ghetto: Donny Hathaway *

BIPOLAR CHRONICLES

314. Little Ghetto Boy: Donny Hathaway *
315. Someday We'll All Be Free: Donny Hathaway *
316. You Were Meant For Me: Donny Hathaway *
317. I Love You More Than You'll Ever Know: Donny Hathaway *
318. To Be Young, Gifted and Black: Donny Hathaway *
319. Season Of the Witch: Donovan
320. A Brighter Day: The Doobie Brothers
321. Long Train Runnin' : The Doobie Brothers
322. Listen To the Music: The Doobie Brothers
323. Takin' It to the Streets: The Doobie Brothers
324. Rockin' Down the Highway: The Doobie Brothers
325. Jesus Is Just Alright: The Doobie Brothers
326. It Keeps You Runnin' : The Doobie Brothers
327. South City Midnight Lady: The Doobie Brothers
328. Take Me In Your Arms: The Doobie Brothers
329. Here To Love You: The Doobie Brothers
330. What A Fool Believes: The Doobie Brothers
331. Another Park Another Sunday: The Doobie Brothers
332. The Captain and Me: The Doobie Brothers
333. Eyes Of Silver: The Doobie Brothers
334. Black Water: The Doobie Brothers
335. Song To See You Through: The Doobie Brothers
336. Spirit: The Doobie Brothers
337. Tell Me What You Want: The Doobie Brothers
338. Neil's Fandango: The Doobie Brothers
339. Love Street: The Doors
340. Love Her Madly: The Doors
341. Touch Me: The Doors
342. L.A. Woman: The Doors

343. Break On Through: The Doors
344. Riders On the Storm: The Doors
345. Love Me Two Times: The Doors
346. Light My Fire: The Doors
347. People Are Strange: The Doors
348. Hello, I Love You: The Doors
349. Waiting For the Sun: The Doors
350. Roadhouse Blues: The Doors
351. God's Plan: Drake
352. Hold On, We're Going Home (feat. Majid Jordan) : Drake
353. Pull Me Under: Dream Theater
354. Hallucinate: Dua Lipa
355. Electricity (feat. Diplo & Mark Ronson) : Silk City, Dua Lipa
356. Be the One: Dua Lipa
357. No Lie (feat. Dua Lipa) : Sean Paul
358. Blow Your Mind: Dua Lipa
359. Hotter Than Hell: Dua Lipa
360. One Kiss: Calvin Harris, Dua Lipa
361. August Town: Duane Stephenson *
362. Heaven Will Rise Up: Duane Stephenson *
363. Ghetto Pain: Duane Stephenson *
364. Cool Runnings: Duane Stephenson *
365. Chant Love: Duane Stephenson *
366. One Great World: Duane Stephenson *
367. Without You: Duane Stephenson *
368. Love Inna Di City: Duane Stephenson *
369. Fairy Tale: Duane Stephenson *
370. Exhale: Duane Stephenson (feat. Tarrus Riley) *
371. Ordinary World: Duane Stephenson *

372. Come Undone: Duran Duran
373. Rio: Duran Duran
374. Union Of the Snake: Duran Duran
375. Morning In America: Durand Jones & the Indications *
376. Don't You Know: Durand Jones & the Indications *
377. Circles: Durand Jones & the Indications *
378. Long Way Home: Durand Jones & the Indications *
379. Son Of A Preacher Man: Dusty Springfield
380. Tequila Sunrise: The Eagles
381. Take It Easy: The Eagles
382. Already Gone: The Eagles
383. One Of These Nights: The Eagles
384. Take It To the Limit: The Eagles
385. Witchy Woman: The Eagles
386. Hotel California: The Eagles
387. Seven Bridges Road: The Eagles
388. New Kid In Town: The Eagles
389. Hole In the World: The Eagles * *
390. Love Music: Earth, Wind & Fire
391. Fantasy: Earth, Wind & Fire
392. Serpentine Fire: Earth, Wind & Fire
393. Devotion: Earth, Wind & Fire
394. Can't Hide Love: Earth, Wind & Fire
395. Devotion: Earth, Wind & Fire
396. Keep Your Head To the Sky: Earth, Wind & Fire
397. Shining Star: Earth, Wind & Fire
398. That's the Way Of the World: Earth, Wind & Fire
399. Reasons: Earth, Wind & Fire
400. Sing A Song: Earth, Wind & Fire

401. Got to Get You Into My Life: Earth, Wind & Fire
402. Shining Star: Earth, Wind & Fire
403. Let's Groove: Earth, Wind & Fire
404. I'll Write A Song For You: Earth, Wind & Fire
405. Happy Feeling: Earth, Wind & Fire
406. All About Love: Earth, Wind & Fire
407. See the Light: Earth, Wind & Fire
408. Lips Like Sugar: Echo & the Bunnymen
409. The Cutter: Echo & the Bunnymen
410. Cool Kids: Echosmith
411. Peace In Our Time: Eddie Money
412. Two Tickets to Paradise: Eddie Money
413. Think I'm In Love: Eddie Money
414. Walk On Water: Eddie Money
415. I Wanna' Go Back: Eddie Money
416. Free Ride: The Edgar Winter Group
417. Thinking Out Loud: Ed Sheeran
418. Shape Of You: Ed Sheeran
419. Don't: Ed Sheeran
420. War: Edwin Starr * *
421. Mr. Blue Sky: Electric Light Orchestra
422. Power: Ellie Goulding
423. Burn: Ellie Goulding
424. Love I'm Given: Ellie Goulding
425. Love Me Like You Do: Ellie Goulding
426. Slow Grenade: Ellie Goulding
427. Close To Me: Ellie Goulding, Diplo & Swae Lee
428. Anything Could Happen: Ellie Goulding
429. Lights: Ellie Goulding

430. Someone Saved My Life Tonight: Elton John
431. Candle In the Wind: Elton John
432. Your Song: Elton John
433. Goodbye Yellow Brick Road: Elton John
434. Philadelphia Freedom: Elton John
435. Rocket Man: Elton John
436. Daniel: Elton John
437. Bennie and the Jets: Elton John
438. Border Song: Elton John
439. Tiny Dancer: Elton John
440. Burn Down the Mission: Elton John
441. Madman Across the Water: Elton John
442. Blessed: Elton John
443. Fooled Around and Fell In Love: Elvin Bishop
444. (What's So Funny 'Bout) Peace, Love and Understanding: Elvis Costello & the Attractions
445. Best Of My Love: The Emotions
446. High and Low: Empire Of the Sun
447. Two Vines: Empire Of the Sun
448. Alive: Empire Of the Sun
449. DNA: Empire Of the Sun
450. Awakening: Empire Of the Sun
451. I'll Be Around: Empire Of the Sun
452. Celebrate: Empire Of the Sun
453. Friends: Empire Of the Sun
454. Walking On A Dream: Empire Of the Sun
455. Lend Me Some Light: Empire Of the Sun
456. We Are the People: Empire Of the Sun
457. I Confess: The English Beat
458. Save It For Later: The English Beat

459. Mirror In the Bathroom: The English Beat
460. Can't Get Used To Losing You: The English Beat
461. Orinoco Flow: Enya
462. A Little Respect: Erasure
463. Chains Of Love: Erasure
464. Star: Erasure
465. Soldier: Erykah Badu
466. On & On: Erykah Badu
467. Window Seat: Erykah Badu
468. Didn't Cha Know: Erykah Badu
469. Love of My Life (An Ode to Hip Hop) : Erykah Badu (feat. Common)
470. Next Lifetime: Erykah Badu
471. Bag Lady: Erykah Badu (feat. Roy Ayres)
472. Back in the Day: Erykah Badu
473. Other Side of the Game: Erykah Badu
474. The Healer: Erykah Badu
475. Gone Baby, Don't Be Long: Erykah Badu
476. Appletree: Erykah Badu
477. Cleva: Erykah Badu (feat. Roy Ayers Ubiquity)
478. Danger: Erykah Badu
479. Phone Down: Erykah Badu
480. Honey: Erykah Badu
481. 4 Leaf Clover: Erykah Badu
482. A.D. 2000: Erykah Badu
483. In Love With You: Erykah Badu
484. Out My Mind, Just in Time: Erykah Badu
485. Spill the Wine: Eric Burdon & War
486. Tears In Heaven: Eric Clapton
487. Let It Rain: Eric Clapton

488. Layla: Eric Clapton & Derek & the Dominos
489. Knockin' On Heaven's Door: Eric Clapton
490. Wonderful Tonight: Eric Clapton
491. The Core: Eric Clapton
492. Sunshine Of Your Love: Eric Clapton
493. Can't Find My Way Home: Eric Clapton & Steve Winwood
494. Sisters Are Doin' It For Themselves: Eurythmics & Aretha Franklin
495. Here Comes the Rain Again: Eurythmics
496. Sweet Dreams: Eurythmics
497. Kiss You All Over: Exile
498. Breathe: Faith Hill
499. Praise You: Fatboy Slim
500. Criminal: Fiona Apple
501. One Thing Leads to Another: The Fixx
502. Saved By Zero: The Fixx
503. Laurelai: Fleet Foxes
504. Mykonos: Fleet Foxes
505. White Winter Hymnal: Fleet Foxes
506. Third of May: Fleet Foxes
507. He Doesn't Know Why: Fleet Foxes
508. Sun It Rises: Fleet Foxes
509. Ragged Wood: Fleet Foxes
510. You Make Loving Fun: Fleetwood Mac
511. Dreams: Fleetwood Mac
512. Rhiannon: Fleetwood Mac
513. As Long As You Follow: Fleetwood Mac
514. Over My Head: Fleetwood Mac
515. Gypsy: Fleetwood Mac
516. The Chain: Fleetwood Mac

517. Silver Spring: Fleetwood Mac
518. World Turning: Fleetwood Mac
519. I Ran: A Flock of Seagulls
520. Wishing: A Flock of Seagulls
521. Times Like These: Foo Fighters
522. Starrider: Foreigner
523. Feels Like the First Time: Foreigner
524. Waiting For A Girl Like You: Foreigner
525. I Want To Know What Love Is: Foreigner
526. Pumped Up Kicks: Foster the People
527. Ain't no Woman (Like the One I've Got) : The Four Tops
528. It Was A Very Good Year: Frank Sinatra
529. My Way: Frank Sinatra
530. The Power of Love: Frankie Goes to Hollywood
531. Rage Hard: Frankie Goes to Hollywood * *
532. For Heaven's Sake: Frankie Goes to Hollywood
533. Ferry Cross the Mersy: Frankie Goes to Hollywood
534. Relax: Frankie Goes to Hollywood
535. War: Frankie Goes to Hollywood * *
536. Two Tribes: Frankie Goes to Hollywood * *
537. All Right Now: Free
538. Killing Me Softly With His Song: Fugees
539. We Are Young: Fun.
540. Carry On: Fun.
541. Some Nights: Fun.
542. You Dropped a Bomb On Me: The Gap Band
543. Outstanding: The Gap Band
544. Love Is Alive: Gary Wright
545. Dream Weaver: Gary Wright

546. Tenderness: General Public
547. Entangled: Genesis
548. Home By the Sea: Genesis
549. A Trick Of the Tail: Genesis
550. Ripples… : Genesis
551. Squonk: Genesis
552. Man On the Corner: Genesis
553. Faith: George Michael
554. Father Figure: George Michael
555. Freedom! '90 : George Michael
556. Careless Whisper: George Michael
557. Right Down the Line: Gerry Raffrty
558. Until I Fall Away: Gin Blossoms
559. Til l Hear It from You: Gin Blossoms
560. Rhinestone Cowboy: Glen Campbell
561. Get On Your Feet: Gloria Estefan
562. Conga: Gloria Estefan
563. Crazy: Gnarls Barkley
564. Iris: The Goo Goo Dolls
565. Slide: The Googoo Dolls
566. Sundown: Gordon Lightfoot
567. If You Could Read My Mind: Gordon Lightfoot
568. Early Mornin' Rain: Gordon Lightfoot
569. Carefree Highway: Gordon Lightfoot
570. The Wreck Of the Edmund Fitzgerald: Gordon Lightfoot
571. Rainy Day People: Gordon Lightfoot
572. Somebody That I Used to Know: Gotye (feat. Kimbra)
573. Eyes Wide Open: Gotye
574. We're an American Band: Grand Funk

575. Some Kind of Wonderful: Grand Funk
576. Ripple: Grateful Dead
577. Playing In the Band: Grateful Dead
578. Touch of Grey: Grateful Dead
579. Truckin' : Grateful Dead
580. Casey Jones: Grateful Dead
581. Sugar Magnolia: Grateful Dead
582. Fire On the Mountain: Grateful Dead
583. France: Grateful Dead
584. Shakedown Street: Grateful Dead
585. Estimated Prophet: Grateful Dead
586. Sugaree: Grateful Dead
587. Ramble On Rose: Grateful Dead
588. Boulevard Of Broken Dreams: Green Day
589. Wake Me Up When September Ends: Green Day
590. Welcome to Paradise: Green Day
591. Jesus Of Suburbia: Green Day
592. Babylon Too Rough: Gregory Isaacs *
593. Cool Down the Pace: Gregory Isaacs *
594. Slave Master: Gregory Isaacs *
595. Border: Gregory Isaacs *
596. Feeling Irie: Gregory Isaacs *
597. All I Have Is Love: Gregory Isaacs *
598. Age of Man: Greta Van Fleet
599. Watching Over: Greta Van Fleet
600. You're the One: Greta Van Fleet
601. Anthem: Greta Van Fleet
602. American Woman: The Guess Who
603. No Time: The Guess Who

604. No Sugar Tonight: The Guess Who
605. Overloaded: Guided By Voices
606. Paradise City: Guns N' Roses
607. Welcome to the Jungle: Guns N' Roses
608. Sweet Child O' Mine: Guns N' Roses
609. Knockin' On Heaven's Door: Guns N' Roses
610. Live and Let Die: Guns N' Roses
611. November Rain: Guns N' Roses
612. Hollaback Girl: Gwen Stefani
613. Hold You: Gyptian (Major Lazer Remix feat. Major Lazer)
614. If You Don't Know Me By Now: Harold Melvin & The Blue Notes
615. Cat's In the Cradle: Harry Chapin
616. Xyz: Harry Chapin
617. Watermelon Sugar: Harry Styles
618. Sunflower, Volume 6: Harry Styles
619. Golden: Harry Styles
620. Sign of the Times: Harry Styles
621. Canyon Moon: Harry Styles
622. Crazy On You: Heart
623. Magic Man: Heart
624. Dog & Butterfly: Heart
625. Straight On: Heart
626. Dreamboat Annie: Heart
627. Barracuda: Heart
628. The Groove Line: Heat Wave
629. Boogie Nights: Heatwave
630. Imagining What to Do: Helado Negro
631. Seen My Aura: Helado Negro
632. Love Me Always: The Heptones *

633. Hypocrite: The Heptones *
634. Our Day Will Come: The Heptones *
635. My Song: H.E.R.
636. Comfortable: H.E.R.
637. Could've Been: H.E.R. (feat. Bryson Tiller)
638. Best Part: H.E.R. (feat. Daniel Caesar)
639. Sometimes: H.E.R.
640. Every Kind of Way: H.E.R.
641. Slow Down: Skip Marley & H.E.R.
642. Only Wanna Be With You: Hootie & The Blowfish
643. Let Her Cry: Hootie & The Blowfish
644. Hold On: Hootie & The Blowfish
645. Hey Hey What Can I Do? : Hootie & The Blowfish
646. You Sexy Thing: Hot Chocolate
647. Take Me to Church: Hozier
648. Do You Believe In Love: Huey Lewis & The News
649. Don't You Want Me: The Human League
650. The Lebanon: The Human League * *
651. I Love It: Icona Pop (feat. Charli XCX)
652. Fancy: Iggy Azalea (feat. Charli XCX)
653. Believer: Imagine Dragons
654. It's Time: Imagine Dragons
655. Natural: Imagine Dragons
656. I Bet My Life: Imagine Dragons
657. Demons: Imagine Dragons
658. Warriors: Imagine Dragons
659. Roots: Imagine Dragons
660. Gold: Imagine Dragons
661. On Top of the World: Imagine Dragons

662. Drive: Incubus
663. On Without Me: Incubus
664. Wish You Were Here: Incubus
665. Karma, Come Back: Incubus
666. * * * * * *
667. Megalomaniac: Incubus * *
668. Warning: Incubus
669. Closer to Fine: Indigo Girls
670. Blood and Fire: Indigo Girls
671. Kid Fears: Indigo Girls
672. Galileo: Indigo Girls
673. Secure Youself: Indigo Girls
674. Land of Canaan: Indigo Girls
675. The Way I Am: Ingrid Michaelson
676. Need You Tonight: INXS
677. What You Need: INXS
678. Suicide Blonde: INXS
679. Never Tear Us Apart: INXS
680. Disappear: INXS
681. The One Thing: INXS
682. New Sensation: INXS
683. Listen Like Thieves: INXS
684. Mediate: INXS
685. Mystify: INXS
686. Flashdance… What A Feeling: Irene Cara
687. Run to the Hills: Iron Maiden
688. Hallowed Be Thy Name: Iron Maiden
689. That Lady, Pts. 1 & 2: The Isley Brothers
690. Somewhere Over the Rainbow: Israel Kamakawiwo'ole

691. Cool and Calm: Israel Vibration *
692. The 3 R's: Jack Johnson
693. Good People: Jack Johnson **
694. Upside Down: Jack Johnson
695. Sitting, Waiting, Wishing: Jack Johnson
696. Better Together: Jack Johnson
697. You and Your Heart: Jack Johnson
698. Angel: Jack Johnson
699. Dancing Machine: Jackson 5
700. I Want You Back: Jackson 5
701. I'll Be There: Jackson 5
702. Abc: Jackson 5
703. Take It Easy: Jackson Browne
704. Rosie: Jackson Browne
705. Colors Of the Sun: Jackson Browne
706. For Everyman: Jackson Browne
707. That Girl Could Sing: Jackson Browne
708. Boulevard: Jackson Browne
709. Doctor My Eyes: Jackson Browne
710. Rock Me On the Water: Jackson Browne
711. You Love the Thunder: Jackson Browne
712. Running On Empty: Jackson Browne
713. Enjoy Yourself: The Jacksons
714. Before I Leave: Jah Cure *
715. Unconditional Love: Jah Cure *
716. Town Called Malice: The Jam
717. Walk Away: James Gang
718. More Than Friends: James Hype (feat. Kellie-Leigh)
719. Shower the People: James Taylor

720. Sweet Baby James: James Taylor
721. Handy Man: James Taylor
722. Country Road: James Taylor
723. Fire and Rain: James Taylor
724. Carolina In My Mind: James Taylor
725. How Sweet It Is: James Taylor
726. Your Smiling Face: James Taylor
727. Something In the Way She Moves: James Taylor
728. Mexico: James Taylor
729. Mockingbird: Carly Simon & James Taylor
730. Been Caught Stealing: Jane's Addiction
731. Jane Says: Jane's Addiction
732. Three Days: Jane's Addiction
733. Turntables: Janelle Monae
734. I Like That: Janelle Monae
735. Yoga: Janelle Monae
736. Prime Time: Janelle Monae
737. Make Me Feel: Janelle Monae
738. Dance Apocalyptic: Janelle Monae
739. Gabby: The Internet (feat. Janelle Monae)
740. Q.U.E.E.N. : Janelle Monae (feat. Erykah Badu)
741. Dance or Die: Janelle Monae (feat. Saul Willliams) * *
742. Electric Lady: Janelle Monae (feat. Solange)
743. Django Jane: Janelle Monae * *
744. Cold War: Janelle Monae * *
745. Venus Fly: Grimes (feat. Janelle Monae)
746. Pynk: Janelle Monae (feat. Grimes)
747. Givin Em What They Love: Janelle Monae (feat. Prince)
748. What Is Love: Janelle Monae

749. What Have You Done for Me Lately: Janet Jackson
750. That's the Way Love Goes: Janet Jackson
751. Escapade: Janet Jackson
752. Rhythm Nation: Janet Jackson * *
753. If: Janet Jackson
754. Love Will Never Do (Without You) : Janet Jackson
755. Runaway: Janet Jackson
756. Let's Wait Awhile: Janet Jackson
757. Got 'Til It's Gone: Janet Jackson
758. Someone to Call My Lover: Janet Jackson
759. Feedback: Janet Jackson
760. Made for Now: Janet Jackson
761. Miss You Much: Janet Jackson
762. When I Think of You: Janet Jackson
763. The Pleasure Principle: Janet Jackson
764. Alright: Janet Jackson
765. Control: Janet Jackson
766. Black Cat: Janet Jackson
767. Scream: Michael Jackson & Janet Jackson
768. The Best Things in Life Are Free: Luther Vandross & Janet Jackson
769. Whatcha Say: Jason Derulo
770. Ridin' Solo: Jason Derulo
771. In My Head: Jason Derulo
772. The Sky's the Limit: Jason Derulo
773. What If: Jason Derulo
774. Fallen: Jason Derulo
775. Queen of Hearts: Jason Derulo
776. I'm Yours: Jason Mraz
777. I Won't Give Up: Jason Mraz

778. The Remedy: Jason Mraz
779. Have It All: Jason Mraz
780. Lucky: Jason Mraz (feat. Colbie Caillat)
781. You Do You: Jason Mraz
782. Wordplay: Jason Mraz
783. Look For The Good: Jason Mraz
784. You and I Both: Jason Mraz
785. Make It Mine: Jason Mraz
786. Geek In the Pink: Jason Mraz
787. Curbside Prophet: Jason Mraz
788. Wise Woman: Jason Mraz *
789. Thunder Island: Jay Ferguson
790. 93 Million Miles: Jason Mraz
791. Did You Get My Message? : Jason Mraz
792. Waiting for the Sun: The Jayhawks
793. Hallelujah: Jeff Buckley
794. Somebody to Love: Jefferson Airplane
795. White Rabbit: Jefferon Airplane
796. Miracles: Jefferson Starship
797. (I've Had) The Time Of My Life: Jennifer Warnes & Bill Medley
798. Rather Be: Clean Bandit (feat. Jess Glynne)
799. Bang Bang: Jessie J, Ariana Grande & Nicki Minaj
800. Tough Love: Jessie Ware
801. Sweetest Song: Jessie Ware
802. Pieces: Jessie Ware
803. Kind Of … Sometimes … Maybe: Jessie Ware
804. Want Your Feeling: Jessie Ware
805. Champagne Kisses: Jessie Ware
806. Share It All: Jessie Ware

807. Bungle In the Jungle: Jethro Tull
808. You Were Meant for Me: Jewel
809. Vaporiza: Jidenna *
810. Little Wing: The Jimi Hendrix Experiment
811. Hey Joe: The Jimi Hendrix Experiment
812. The Wind Cries Mary: The Jimi Hendrix Experiment
813. Foxey Lady: The Jimi Hendrix Experiment
814. Castles Made Of Sand: The Jimi Hendrix Experiment
815. Purple Haze: The Jimi Hendrix Experiment
816. All Along the Watchtower: The Jimi Hendrix Experiment
817. Crosstown Traffic: The Jimi Hendrix Experiment
818. Angel: The Jimi Hendrix Experiment
819. Manic Depression: The Jimi Hendrix Experiment
820. You Can Get It If You Really Want It: Jimmy Cliff *
821. Many Rivers to Cross: Jimmy Cliff *
822. Wonderful World, Beautiful People: Jimmy Cliff *
823. Hard Road to Travel: Jimmy Cliff *
824. The Harder They Come: Jimmy Cliff *
825. Bongo Man: Jimmy Cliff *
826. I Can See Clearly Now: Jimmy Cliff *
827. Wild World: Jimmy Cliff *
828. Sitting In Limbo: Jimmy Cliff *
829. Vietnam: Jimmy Cliff *
830. Shelter Of Your Love: Jimmy Cliff*
831. Sooner Or Later: Jimmy Cliff *
832. Bongo Man: Jimmy Cliff *
833. Sufferin' In the Land: Jimmy Cliff * *
834. The Middle: Jimmy Eat World
835. Forever Young: Joan Baez

836. Diamonds & Rust: Joan Baez
837. With A Little Help From My Friends: Joe Cocker
838. Breaking Us In Two: Joe Jackson
839. Take Me Home, Country Roads: John Denver
840. Rocky Mountain High: John Denver
841. Calypso: John Denver
842. Actions: John Legend
843. I Do: John Legend
844. One Life: John Legend
845. Number One: John Legend (feat. Kanye West)
846. Let's Get Lifted: John Legend
847. I Can Change: John Legend (feat. Snoop Dogg)
848. Ordinary People: John Legend
849. Stay With You: John Legend
850. Let's Get Lifted Again: John Legend
851. So High: John Legend (feat. Lauryn Hill)
852. Live It Up: John Legend (feat. Miri Ben-Ari)
853. Refuge: John Legend
854. Focused: John Legend
855. Bigger Love: John Legend
856. Conversations in the Dark: John Legend
857. Always: John Legend
858. Cherry Bomb: John Mellencamp
859. Jack & Diane: John Mellencamp
860. Pink Houses: John Mellencamp
861. Authority Song: John Mellencamp
862. Crumblin' Down: John Mellencamp
863. Rain On the Scarecrow: John Mellencamp
864. Peaceful World: John Mellencamp

865. Love and Happiness: John Mellencamp * *
866. Ring of Fire: Johnny Cash
867. Cruel Crazy Beautiful World: Johnny Clegg * *
868. Great Heart: Johnny Clegg & Savuka * *
869. Dela: Johnny Clegg & Savuka *
870. Siyayilanda: Johnny Clegg & Savuka *
871. One (Hu)Man One Vote: Johnny Clegg & Savuka * *
872. The Crossing (Osiyeza) : Johnny Clegg & Savuka *
873. Take My Heart Away: Johnny Clegg & Savuka *
874. I Call Your Name: Johnny Clegg & Savuka *
875. Third World Child: Johnny Clegg & Savuka * *
876. Tough Enough: Johnny Clegg & Savuka *
877. These Days: Johnny Clegg & Savuka *
878. In My African Dream: Johnny Clegg & Savuka *
879. Africa (What Made You So Strong) : Johnny Clegg & Savuka * *
880. I Can See Clearly Now: Johnny Nash
881. Rise: Jonas Blue (feat. Jack & Jack) * *
882. Polaroid: Jonas Blue, Liam Payne & Lennon Stella *
883. Cool: Jonas Brothers
884. River: Joni Mitchell
885. Cool Water: Joni Mitchell
886. Carey: Joni Mitchell
887. Court and Spark: Joni Mitchell
888. Help Me: Joni Mitchell
889. Free Man in Paris: Joni Mitchell
890. People's Parties: Joni Mitchell
891. Same Situation: Joni Mitchell
892. Car on a Hill: Joni Mitchell
893. Down to You: Joni Mitchell

894. Raised on Robbery: Joni Mitchell
895. Woodstock: Joni Mitchell
896. The Circle Game: Joni Mitchell
897. Cold Blue Steel and Sweet Fire: Joni Mitchell
898. Ladies of the Canyon: Joni Mitchell
899. Banquet: Joni Mitchell
900. Barandgrill: Joni Mitchell
901. See You Sometime: Joni Mitchell
902. Electricity: Joni Mitchell
903. You Turn Me On I'm a Radio: Joni Mitchell
904. Blonde In the Bleachers: Joni Mitchell
905. Let the Wind Carry Me: Joni Mitchell
906. Don't Stop Believin': Journey
907. Lovin', Touchin', Squeezin': Journey
908. Only the Young: Journey
909. Lights: Journey
910. Daydream: Journey
911. When You're Alone (It Ain't Easy) : Journey
912. Too Late: Journey
913. Love Will Tear Us Apart: Joy Division
914. Move Your Feet: Junior Senior
915. Anticipation: Justine Skye (feat. Kranium)
916. Mirrors: Justin Timberlake
917. Cry Me A River: Justin Timberlake
918. Rock Your Body: Justin Timberlake
919. Take Back the Night: Justin Timberlake
920. Suit & Tie: Justin Timberlake (feat. JAY-Z)
921. That Girl: Justin Timberlake
922. Too Shy: Kajagoogoo

923. Carry On Wayward Son: Kansas
924. Dust In the Wind: Kansas
925. Point Of No Return: Kansas
926. Hold On: Kansas
927. Portrait: Kansas
928. Play the Game Tonight: Kansas
929. All of the Lights: Kanye West
930. Down With You: Katchafire *
931. Feels Like: Katchafire *
932. Seriously: Katchafire *
933. Love Letter: Katchafire *
934. Walking on Sunshine: Katrina & The Waves
935. I Kissed a Girl: Katy Perry
936. Roar: Katy Perry
937. Firework: Katy Perry
938. Wide Awake: Katy Perry
939. Get Down Tonight: KC and The Sunshine Band
940. Somewhere Only We Know: Keane
941. Since U Been Gone: Kelly Clarkson
942. Because of You: Kelly Clarkson * *
943. Miss Independent: Kelly Clarkson
944. Alright: Kendrick Lamar * *
945. What A Fool Believes: Kenny Loggins & Michael McDonald
946. Blue On Black: Kenny Wayne Shepherd Band
947. All Summer Long: Kid Rock
948. Run for Cover: The Killers * *
949. Use Somebody: Kings of Leon
950. Revolution: Kirk Franklin & The Family * *
951. Brighter Day: Kirk Franklin

952. Melodies from Heaven: Kirk Franklin
953. God of Thunder: Kiss
954. Cut Yr Teeth: Kississippi
955. Celebration: Kool & The Gang
956. Jungle Boogie: Kool & The Gang
957. Hollywood Swinging: Kool & The Gang
958. Can't Believe (feat. Ty Dolla $ign & WizKid): Kranium *
959. Through the Window: Kranium *
960. Black Horse and the Cherry Tree: KT Tunstall
961. Suddenly I See: KT Tunstall
962. Other Side of the World: KT Tunstall
963. Strange Sight: KT Tunstall
964. All the Lovers: Kylie Minogue
965. Magic: Kylie Minogue
966. Light Years: Kylie Minogue
967. On a Night Like This: Kylie Minogue
968. Can't Get You Out of My Head: Kylie Minogue
969. Get Outta My Way: Kylie Minogue
970. Wow: Kylie Minogue
971. Magic (Purple Disco Machine Remix) : Kylie Minogue
972. I Love It: Kylie Minogue
973. Spinning Around: Kylie Minogue
974. Say Something: Kylie Minogue
975. Love at First Sight: Kylie Minogue
976. Can't Beat the Feeling: Kylie Minogue
977. Saddle Up: L.M.S. (feat. Morgan Heritage) * *
978. Lady Marmalade: LaBelle
979. Need You Now: Lady Antebellum
980. Applause: Lady Gaga

981. Marry the Night: Lady Gaga
982. Born This Way: Lady Gaga
983. The Edge of Glory: Lady Gaga
984. Just Dance: Lady Gaga (feat. Colby O'Donis)
985. Paparazzi: Lady Gaga
986. Poker Face: Lady Gaga
987. Monster: Lady Gaga
988. Telephone: Lady Gaga (feat. Beyonce)
989. Million Reasons: Lady Gaga
990. Til It Happens To You: Lady Gaga
991. Summertime Sadness: Lana Del Rey & Cedric Gervais
992. Hold Me Closer: LANKS
993. Aurelia: LANKS
994. Beach Houses: LANKS
995. Settle Down: LANKS
996. Brothers of the Mountain: LANKS
997. Whale Song: LANKS
998. Bitter Leaf: LANKS
999. Brave Man: LANKS
1000. Spiritual Man: LANKS
1001. My Own Mystery: LANKS (feat. Ngaiire)
1002. Rebound: LANKS (feat. Nick Hill & JANEVA)
1003. Green Light: LANKS
1004. Knife and Spear: LANKS
1005. Ex-Factor: Lauryn Hill
1006. Doo Wop (That Thing) : Lauryn Hill
1007. Can't Take My Eyes Off You: Lauryn Hill
1008. Every Ghetto, Every City: Lauryn Hill * *
1009. Forgive Them Father: Lauryn Hill * *

1010. Everything Is Everything: Lauryn Hill Lauryn Hill
1011. To Zion: Lauryn Hill (feat. Carlos Santana)
1012. Lost Ones: Lauryn Hill * *
1013. Superstar: Lauryn Hill
1014. Final Hour: Lauryn Hill
1015. When It Hurts so Bad: Lauryn Hill
1016. I Used to Love Him: Lauryn Hill (feat. Mary J. Blige)
1017. Nothing Even Matters: Lauryn Hill (feat. D'Angelo)
1018. Tell Him: Lauryn Hill
1019. Sound of Silver: LCD Soundsystem
1020. I Can Change: LCD Soundsystem
1021. Hey Hey What Can I Do: Led Zeppelin
1022. Stairway to Heaven: Led Zeppelin
1023. Kashmir: Led Zeppelin
1024. The Song Remains the Same: Led Zeppelin
1025. The Rain Song: Led Zeppelin
1026. Over the Hills and Far Away: Led Zeppelin
1027. The Crunge: Led Zeppelin
1028. Dancing Days: Led Zeppelin
1029. D'yer Mak'er: Led Zeppelin
1030. No Quarter: Led Zeppelin
1031. Carouselambra: Led Zeppelin
1032. Good Times Bad Times: Led Zeppelin
1033. Dazed and Confused: Led Zeppelin
1034. Your Time Is Gonna Come: Led Zeppelin
1035. Whole Lotta Love: Led Zeppelin
1036. What is and What Should Never Be: Led Zeppelin
1037. Thank You: Led Zeppelin
1038. Going to California: Led Zeppelin

1039. Living Loving Maid: Led Zeppelin
1040. Ramble On: Led Zeppelin
1041. Immigrant Song: Led Zeppelin
1042. Gallows Pole: Led Zeppelin
1043. Tangerine: Led Zeppelin
1044. When the Levee Breaks: Led Zeppelin
1045. Misty Mountain Hop: Led Zeppelin
1046. Over the Hills and Far Away: Led Zeppelin
1047. I Hope You Dance: Lee Ann Womack
1048. Fly Away: Lenny Kravitz
1049. Are You Gonna Go My Way: Lenny Kravitz
1050. American Woman: Lenny Kravitz
1051. Let Love Rule: Lenny Kravitz
1052. Always On the Run: Lenny Kravitz
1053. Lady: Lenny Kravitz
1054. Believe: Lenny Kravitz
1055. I Belong to You: Lenny Kravitz
1056. Stand By My Woman: Lenny Kravitz
1057. I'll Be Waiting: Lenny Kravitz
1058. Heaven Help: Lenny Kravitz
1059. When I Need You: Leo Sayer
1060. Better In Time: Leona Lewis
1061. Here and Now: Letters to Cleo
1062. You're No Good: Linda Ronstadt
1063. In the End: LINKIN PARK
1064. Somewhere I Belong: LINKIN PARK
1065. One Step Closer: LINKIN PARK
1066. What I've Done: LINKIN PARK
1067. Breaking the Habit: LINKIN PARK

1068. The Catalyst: LINKIN PARK
1069. BURN IT DOWN: LINKIN PARK
1070. All Night Long: Lionel Richie
1071. Stuck On You: Lionel Richie (feat. Darius Rucker)
1072. You Are: Lionel Richie
1073. Black Magic: Little Mix
1074. Wings: Little Mix
1075. Rock Anthem: LMFAO (feat. Lauren Bennett & GoonRock)
1076. Vahevala: Loggins & Messina
1077. House at Pooh Corner: Loggins & Messina
1078. Watching the River Run: Loggins & Messina
1079. Angry Eyes: Loggins & Messina
1080. Be Free: Loggins & Messina
1081. Brandy: Looking Glass
1082. Royals: Lorde
1083. Heaven: Los Lonely Boys
1084. Turn Me Loose: Loverboy
1085. Do You Believe In Magic? : The Lovin' Spoonful
1086. To Sir With Love: Lulu
1087. Never Too Much: Luther Vandross
1088. Always and Forever: Luther Vandross
1089. Gimme Back My Bullets: Lynyrd Skynyrd
1090. Saturday Night Special: Lynyrd Skynyrd
1091. Simple Man: Lynyrd Skynyrd
1092. Free Bird: Lynyrd Skynyrd
1093. Sweet Home Alabama: Lynyrd Skynyrd
1094. Tuesday's Gone: Lynyrd Skynyrd
1095. What's Your Name: Lynyrd Skynyrd
1096. Our House: Madness

1097. Take A Bow: Madonna
1098. Like A Prayer: Madonna
1099. Express Yourself: Madonna
1100. Crazy for You: Madonna
1101. Holiday: Madonna
1102. Lucky Star: Madonna
1103. Borderline: Madonna
1104. Into the Groove: Madonna
1105. La Isla Bonita: Madonna
1106. Vogue: Madonna
1107. Papa Don't Preach: Madonna
1108. Music: Madonna
1109. Express Yourself: Madonna
1110. Ray of Light: Madonna
1111. Live to Tell: Madonna
1112. Beautiful Stranger: Madonna
1113. Blinded By the light: Manfred Mann's Earth Band
1114. Dreamlover: Mariah Carey
1115. Moves Like Jagger: Maroon 5
1116. She Will Be Loved: Maroon 5
1117. Sugar: Maroon 5
1118. Sex and Candy: Maroon 5
1119. If I Never See Your Face Again: Maroon 5 (feat. Rihanna)
1120. Can't You See: The Marshall Tucker Band
1121. Happier: Marshmello & Bastille
1122. High on Life: Martin Garrix (feat. Bonn)
1123. Places: Martin Solveig (feat. Ina Wroldsen)
1124. Got to Give It Up: Marvin Gaye
1125. What's Going On: Marvin Gaye

1126. Let's Get It On: Marvin Gaye

1127. Mercy Mercy Me: Marvin Gaye

1128. I Want You: Marvin Gaye

1129. Safe from Harm: Massive Attack

1130. 3 am: Matchbox Twenty

1131. Sunday Morning: Matoma (feat. Josie Dunne)

1132. Joy and Pain: Maze & Frankie Beverly

1133. Ain't No Stoppin' Us Now: McFadden & Whitehead

1134. All About That Bass: Meghan Trainor

1135. You Can Sleep While I Drive: Melissa Etheridge

1136. Breathe: Melissa Etheridge

1137. Bring Me Some Water: Melissa Etheridge

1138. I'm the Only One: Melissa Etheridge

1139. Come To My Window: Melissa Etheridge

1140. Silent Legacy: Melissa Etheridge

1141. I Will Never Be the Same: Melissa Etheridge

1142. All American Girl: Melissa Etheridge

1143. Yes I Am: Melissa Etheridge

1144. Resist: Melissa Etheridge

1145. Talking To My Angel: Melissa Etheridge

1146. Ruins: Melissa Etheridge

1147. Down Under: Melissa Etheridge

1148. Down By the Sea: Melissa Etheridge

1149. Enter Sandman: Metallica

1150. The Unforgiven: Metallica

1151. For Whom the Bell Tolls: Metallica

1152. Nothing Else Matters: Metallica

1153. Wherever I May Roam: Metallica

1154. Kids: MGMT

1155. Mad World: Michael Andrews (feat. Gary Jules)

1156. Say Hey (I Love You) : Michael Franti & Spearhead (feat. Cherine Tanya Anderson)

1157. Rock With You: Michael Jackson

1158. P.Y.T. (Pretty Young Thing) : Michael Jackson

1159. Thriller: Michael Jackson

1160. The Way You Make Me Feel: Michael Jackson

1161. Man In the Mirror: Michael Jackson

1162. Dirty Diana: Michael Jackson

1163. Black or White: Michael Jackson * *

1164. Wanna Be Startin' Somethin' : Michael Jackson

1165. Billie Jean: Michael Jackson

1166. Human Nature: Michael Jackson

1167. This Is It: Michael Jackson

1168. Workin' Day and Night: Michael Jackson

1169. I Keep Forgettin: Michael McDonald

1170. Mistake: Middle Kids

1171. All I Need Is a Miracle: Mike + The Mechanics

1172. I Took a Pill in Ibiza: Mike Posner

1173. Destination Unknown: Missing Persons

1174. Walking in L.A. : Missing Persons

1175. Words: Missing Persons

1176. Back & Forth: MK, Jonas Blue & Becky Hill

1177. Porcelain: Moby

1178. Why Does My Heart Feel So Bad? : Moby

1179. South Side: Moby

1180. Go: Moby

1181. Power Is Taken: Moby * *

1182. I Melt With You: Modern English

1183. I'm a Believer: The Monkees

1184. Rock the Nation: Montrose
1185. Rock Candy: Montrose
1186. Bad Motor Scooter: Montrose
1187. Nights In White Satin: The Moody Blues
1188. Lost Heads: Moon Duo
1189. Eye 2 Eye: Moon Duo
1190. Fever Night: Moon Duo
1191. Eternal Shore: Moon Duo
1192. The World and the Sun: Moon Duo
1193. Stars Are the Light: Moon Duo
1194. Flying: Moon Duo
1195. Light It Up: Morgan Heritage (feat. Jo Mersa Marley) * *
1196. Jah Comes First: Morgan Heritage *
1197. One Day: Morgan Heritage *
1198. Rise and Fall: Morgan Heritage *
1199. So Amazing: Morgan Heritage *
1200. Wanna Be Loved: Morgan Heritage *
1201. We Are Warriors: Morgan Heritage * *
1202. Sunday Morning: Morgan Heritage *
1203. Celebrate Life: Morgan Heritage *
1204. Come Fly: Morgan Heritage (feat. Flogging Molly) *
1205. Rise Up: Morgan Heritage * *
1206. Lion Order: Morgan Heritage *
1207. Sing Your Life: Morrissey
1208. Young & Unafraid: The Moth & The Flame
1209. Live While I Breathe: The Moth & The Flame
1210. Kyrie: Mr. Mister
1211. Silver Lining: Mt. Joy
1212. I Will Wait: Mumford & Sons

1213. Lover of the Light: Mumford & Sons
1214. Year of the Tiger: Myles Kennedy
1215. I Can: Nas
1216. So Sick: Ne-Yo
1217. Push Back: Ne-Yo, Bebe Rexha & Stefflon Don
1218. Solitary Man: Neil Diamond
1219. Shilo: Neil Diamond
1220. Crunchy Granola Suite: Neil Diamond
1221. Play Me: Neil Diamond
1222. Sweet Caroline: Neil Diamond
1223. Cracklin' Rose: Neil Diamond
1224. Brooklyn Roads: Neil Diamond
1225. Soolaimon: Neil Diamond
1226. Holly Holy: Neil Diamond
1227. Cinnamon Girl: Neil Young
1228. Needle and the Damage Done: Neil Young
1229. After the Gold Rush: Neil Young
1230. Old Man: Neil Young
1231. Heart of Gold: Neil Young
1232. Ohio: Neil Young
1233. Hey Hey, My My: Neil Young
1234. Down by the River: Neil Young
1235. Sugar Mountain: Neil Young
1236. Long May You Run: Neil Young
1237. Cowgirl In the Sand: Neil Young
1238. When You Dance: Neil Young
1239. Comes A Time: Neil Young
1240. Southern Man: Neil Young * *
1241. I'm Like A Bird: Nelly Furtado

1242. World (Perfecto Mix) : New Order
1243. Bizarre Love Triangle: New Order
1244. True Faith: New Order
1245. How You Remind Me: Nickelback
1246. Feed the Machine: Nickelback
1247. Song on Fire: Nickelback
1248. Must Be Nice: Nickelback
1249. Rockstar: Nickelback
1250. Someday: Nickelback
1251. Photograph: Nickelback
1252. If Today Was Your Last Day: Nickelback
1253. When We Stand Together: Nickelback
1254. Far Away: Nickelback
1255. Super Bass: Nicki Minaj
1256. Don't Tell Me You Love Me: Night Ranger
1257. Sister Christian: Night Ranger
1258. Smells Like Teen Spirit: Nirvana
1259. Lithium: Nirvana
1260. Come As You Are: Nirvana
1261. All Apologies: Nirvana
1262. Heart-Shaped Box: Nirvana
1263. Hella Good: No Doubt
1264. Underneath It All: No Doubt (feat. Lady Saw)
1265. Just A Girl: No Doubt
1266. Don't Speak: No Doubt
1267. Wonderwall: Oasis
1268. Champagne Supernova: Oasis
1269. Back Stabbers: The O'Jays
1270. Love Train: The O'Jays

1271. I Love Music: The O'Jays

1272. For the Love of Money: The O'Jays

1273. Love Rollercoaster: Ohio Players

1274. Fire: Ohio Players

1275. Dead Man's Party: Oingo Boingo

1276. Only A Lad: Oingo Boingo

1277. Just Another Day: Oingo Boingo

1278. Who Do You Want to Be: Oingo Boingo

1279. Story Of My Life: One Direction

1280. Diana: One Direction

1281. If You Only Knew: One Drop *

1282. Daniel in the Lion's Den: One Drop *

1283. Forward: One Drop *

1284. Counting Stars: OneRepublic

1285. Apologize: OneRepublic

1286. Wherever I Go: OneRepublic

1287. Rip It Up: Orange Juice *

1288. Angel of Music: Sarah Brightman & Janet Devenish

1289. Still the One: Orleans

1290. Hey Ya! : Outkast

1291. Rock All Day: Outlandish

1292. Feels Like Saving the World: Outkast

1293. Always Remember: Outlandish

1294. Keep the Record On Play: Outlandish

1295. Let Off Some Steam: Outlandish

1296. Feels Like Saving the World: Outlandish

1297. Amen: Outlandish

1298. Someday: Outlandish

1299. Sound of a Rebel: Outlandish

1300. Ready to Love: Outlandish
1301. Hurry Sundown: The Outlaws
1302. Green Grass and High Tides Forever: The Outlaws
1303. Comes a Time: The Outlaws
1304. There Goes Another Love Song: The Outlaws
1305. Breaker Breaker: The Outlaws
1306. You Are the Show: The Outlaws
1307. (Ghost) Riders in the Sky: The Outlaws
1308. Song in the Breeze: The Outlaws
1309. Holiday: The Outlaws
1310. Night Wines: The Outlaws
1311. Jackie Blue: The Ozark Mountain Daredevils
1312. Crazy Train: Ozzy Osbourne
1313. I Don't Know: Ozzy Osbourne
1314. Mr. Crowley: Ozzy Osbourne
1315. Over the Mountain: Ozzy Osbourne
1316. Shot In the Dark: Ozzy Osbourne
1317. Mama, I'm Coming Home: Ozzy Osbourne
1318. Raise Your Glass: Pink
1319. Just Give Me a Reason: Pink
1320. Flashlight: Parliament
1321. Give up the Funk: Parliament
1322. Let Her Go: Passenger
1323. Invincible: Pat Benatar
1324. Hell Is for Children: Pat Benatar * *
1325. Love Is a Battlefield: Pat Benatar
1326. We Belong: Pat Benatar
1327. You Better Run: Pat Benatar
1328. Promises in the Dark: Pat Benatar

1329. Shadows of the Night: Pat Benatar

1330. Where Have All the Cowboys Gone? : Paula Cole

1331. I Go Crazy: Paul Davis

1332. Still Crazy After All These Years: Paul Simon

1333. Listen to What the Man Said: Wings

1334. Live and Let Die: Wings

1335. Silly Love Songs: Wings

1336. Uncle Albert/Admiral Halsey: Paul McCartney & Wings

1337. Jet: Paul McCartney & Wings

1338. Band on the Run: Paul McCartney & Wings

1339. Graceland: Paul McCartney

1340. You Can Call Me Al: Paul McCartney

1341. Late In the Evening: Paul McCartney

1342. Slip Slidin' Away: Paul McCartney

1343. Mother and Child Reunion: Paul McCartney

1344. My Little Town: Paul McCartney

1345. Kodachrome: Paul McCartney

1346. New York: Paul Weller

1347. One Tear: Paul Weller

1348. Here: Pavement

1349. Spit on a Stranger: Pavement

1350. Nothing As It Seems: Pearl Jam

1351. Black: Pearl Jam

1352. Love, Reign O'er Me: Pearl Jam

1353. Alive: Pearl Jam

1354. Even Flow: Pearl Jam

1355. Jeremy: Pearl Jam

1356. Daughter: Pearl Jam

1357. Just Breathe: Pearl Jam

1358. Yellow Ledbetter: Pearl Jam
1359. Corduroy: Pearl Jam
1360. Once: Pearl Jam
1361. Garden: Pearl Jam
1362. Love You Long Time: Pentatonix
1363. Hallelujah: Pentatonix
1364. We Are Young: Pentatonix
1365. Aha! : Pentatonix
1366. Bohemian Rhapsody: Pentatonix
1367. Imagine: Pentatonix
1368. Little Drummer Boy: Pentatonix
1369. Show You How to Love: Pentatonix
1370. TalkTalk: A Perfect Circle
1371. What Have I Done To Deserve This (with Dusty Springfield) : Pet Shop Boys
1372. West End Girls: Pet Shop Boys
1373. Go West: Pet Shop Boys
1374. Show Me the Way: Peter Frampton
1375. Baby, I Love Your Way: Peter Frampton
1376. Do You Feel Like We Do? : Peter Frampton
1377. Solsbury Hill: Peter Gabriel
1378. Games Without Frontiers: Peter Gabriel
1379. Sledgehammer: Peter Gabriel
1380. In Your Eyes: Peter Gabriel
1381. Major Tom: Peter Gabriel
1382. Not Gonna Give It Up: Peter Tosh *
1383. Stop That Train: Peter Tosh *
1384. Where You Gonna Run: Peter Tosh *
1385. Peace Treaty: Peter Tosh * *
1386. Feel No Way: Peter Tosh *

1387. I Dig Rock and Roll Music: Peter, Paul & Mary

1388. Leaving On a Jet Plane: Peter, Paul & Mary

1389. Puff, The Magic Dragon: Peter, Paul & Mary

1390. Blowin' In the Wind: Peter, Paul & Mary * *

1391. If I Had a Hammer: Peter, Paul & Mary * *

1392. Early Mornin' Rain: Peter, Paul & Mary

1393. Lemon Tree: Peter, Paul & Mary

1394. This Land Is Your Land: Peter, Paul & Mary

1395. Downtown: Petula Clark

1396. Happy: Pharrell Williams

1397. Freedom: Pharrell Williams

1398. Entrepreneur (feat. JAY-Z) : Pharrell Williams

1399. Drop It Like It's Hot (feat. Pharrell Williams) : Snoop Dogg

1400. Come Get It Bae: Pharrell Williams

1401. Frontin' (feat. JAY-Z) : Pharrell Williams

1402. That Girl: Pharrell Williams & Snoop Dogg

1403. Blurred Line (feat. T.I. & Pharrell) : Robin Thicke

1404. Angel: Pharrell Williams

1405. Marilyn Monroe: Pharrell Williams

1406. In the Air Tonight: Pharrell Williams

1407. Devotion to a Dream: Phish

1408. Sigma Oasis: Phish

1409. Free: Phish

1410. Bouncing Around the Room: Phish

1411. Sample In a Jar: Phish

1412. Farmhouse: Phish

1413. Pigs (Three Different Ones) : Pink Floyd

1414. Dogs: Pink Floyd

1415. Sheep: Pink Floyd

1416. Wish You Were Here: Pink Floyd

1417. On the Turning Away: Pink Floyd * *

1418. Welcome to the Machine: Pink Floyd

1419. Goodbye Blue Sky: Pink Floyd

1420. Comfortably Numb: Pink Floyd

1421. Shine On You Crazy Diamond: Pink Floyd

1422. Have a Cigar: Pink Floyd

1423. Baby Come Back: Player

1424. A Million Miles Away: The Plimsouls

1425. Go Bang (feat. Kira Divine) : PNAU

1426. Yes, We Can, Can: The Pointer Sisters

1427. I'm So Excited: The Pointer Sisters

1428. Jump (For My Love) : The Pointer Sisters

1429. Neutron Dance: The Pointer Sisters

1430. Fire: The Pointer Sisters

1431. He's So Shy: The Pointer Sisters

1432. Spirits in the Material World: The Police

1433. Synchronicity I: The Police

1434. Driven to Tears: The Police

1435. Walking On the Moon: The Police

1436. Roxanne: The Police The Police

1437. Every Little Thing She Does Is Magic: The Police

1438. De Do Do Do, De Da Da Da: The Police

1439. Wrapped Around Your Finger: The Police

1440. Message in a Bottle: The Police

1441. Don't Stand So Close to Me: The Police

1442. Synchronicity II: The Police

1443. Invisible Sun: The Police

1444. Bombs Away: The Police * *

1445. Hollywood's Bleeding: Post Malone
1446. Circles: Post Malone
1447. A Thousand Bad Times: Post Malone
1448. Staring at the Sun: Post Malone
1449. Die For Me (feat. Future & Halsey) : Post Malone
1450. On the Road (feat. Meek Mill & Lil Baby) : Post Malone
1451. Sunflower: Post Malone & Swae Lee
1452. Rise Today: Pressure * *
1453. Show Love: Pressure *
1454. Stand Firm: Pressure *
1455. Cry for Humanity (feat. Ras Batch & Niyorah) : Pressure * *
1456. Who You Are: Pressure * *
1457. Serious About It: Pressure *
1458. Run Away: Pressure *
1459. The Rain: Pressure *
1460. The Sound: Pressure *
1461. Hail the King of Kings: Pressure *
1462. Nothing No Wrong (feat. Midnite) : Pressure *
1463. I'll Stand By You: Pretenders
1464. My City Was Gone: Pretenders
1465. Middle of the Road: Pretenders
1466. Back On the Chain Gang: Pretenders
1467. Mystery Acheivement: Pretenders
1468. Cuban Slide: Pretenders
1469. I'll Stand By You: Pretenders
1470. Talk of the Town: Pretenders
1471. I Got You Babe (feat. Chrissie Hynde) : UB40
1472. Love My Way: The Psychedelic Furs
1473. Heartbreak Beat: The Psychedelic Furs

1474. Pretty In Pink: The The Psychedelic Furs
1475. Heaven: The Psychedelic Furs
1476. Mr. Jones: The Psychedelic Furs
1477. All That Money Wants: The Psychedelic Furs
1478. The Ghost In You: The Psychedelic Furs
1479. Fight the Power: Public Enemy * *
1480. Amie: Pure Prairie League
1481. Bohemian Rhapsody: Queen
1482. We Are the Champions: Queen
1483. Crazy Little Thing Called Love: Queen
1484. We Will Rock You: Queen
1485. You're My Best Friend: Queen
1486. The Prophet's Song: Queen
1487. Another One Bites the Dust: Queen
1488. Somebody to Love: Queen
1489. A Kind of Magic: Queen
1490. I'm Going Slightly Mad: Queen
1491. Silent Lucidity: Queensryche
1492. Empire: Queensryche * *
1493. Karma Police: Radiohead
1494. Talk Show Host: Radiohead
1495. Killing In the Name: Rage Against the Machine * *
1496. Man On the Silver Mountain: Rainbow
1497. I Just Want to Celebrate: Rare Earth
1498. Santa Barbara: Rebelution *
1499. Inhale Exhale (feat. Protoje) : Rebelution *
1500. High on Life: Rebelution *
1501. Those Days: Rebelution *
1502. Free up Your Mind: Rebelution *

1503. Breakdown: Rebelution *

1504. Higher Ground: Red Hot Chili Peppers

1505. Under the Bridge: Red Hot Chili Peppers

1506. Californication: Red Hot Chili Peppers

1507. Otherside: Red Hot Chili Peppers

1508. Scar Tissue: Red Hot Chili Peppers

1509. Orange Crush: R.E.M. * *

1510. It's the End of the World As We Know It: R.E.M.

1511. Man on the Moon: R.E.M.

1512. Ignoreland: R.E.M.

1513. The Sidewinder Sleeps Tonite: R.E.M.

1514. Fall On Me: R.E.M.

1515. Radio Free Europe: R.E.M.

1516. Shiny Happy People: R.E.M.

1517. Ridin' the Storm Out: REO Speedwagon

1518. Time for Me to Fly: REO Speedwagon

1519. Roll with the Changes: REO Speedwagon

1520. Keep on Loving You: REO Speedwagon

1521. Can't Fight This Feeling: REO Speedwagon

1522. Give It to Me Baby: Rick James

1523. Livin' la Vida Loca: Ricky Martin

1524. Garden Party: Ricky Nelson

1525. Unchained Melody: The Righteous Brothers

1526. Work (feat. Drake) : Rihanna

1527. Diamonds: Rihanna

1528. Don't Stop the Music: Rihanna

1529. Only Girl (In the World) : Rihanna

1530. We Found Love (feat. Calvin Harris) : Rihanna

1531. Stay (feat. Mikky Ekko) : Rihanna

1532. It Takes Two: Rob Base & DJ EZ Rock
1533. Angels: Robbie Williams
1534. Ship of Fools: Robert Plant
1535. In the Mood: Robert Plant
1536. Song to the Siren: Robert Plant
1537. Tall Cool One: Robert Plant
1538. Rainbow: Robert Plant
1539. Forever Young: Rod Stewart
1540. Maggie May: Rod Stewart
1541. Mandolin Wind: Rod Stewart
1542. Tonight's the Night: Rod Stewart
1543. You're In My Heart: Rod Stewart
1544. Downtown Train: Rod Stewart
1545. Gimme Shelter: The Rolling Stones
1546. Angie: The Rolling Stones
1547. Sympathy for the Devil: The Rolling Stones
1548. Wild Horses: The Rolling Stones
1549. Honky Tonk Women: The Rolling Stones
1550. Tumbling Dice: The Rolling Stones
1551. Ray of Sunshine: Romain Virgo *
1552. Fantasize: Romain Virgo *
1553. Don't You Remember: Romain Virgo *
1554. Mama's Song: Romain Virgo *
1555. Car Wash: Rose Royce
1556. It Must Have Been Love: Roxette
1557. Crash! Boom! Bang! : Roxette
1558. Avalon: Roxy Music
1559. More Than This: Roxy Music
1560. The Main Thing: Roxy Music

1561. To Turn You On: Roxy Music
1562. New World Man: Roxy Music
1563. True to Life: Roxy Music
1564. Eight Miles High: Roxy Music
1565. Tell Me Something Good: Rufus
1566. Limelight: Rush
1567. Tom Sawyer: Rush
1568. The Sweetest Taboo: Sade
1569. No Ordinary Love: Sade
1570. Smooth Operator: Sade
1571. Your Love Is King: Sade
1572. Paradise: Sade
1573. Immigrant: Sade
1574. By Your Side: Sade
1575. La La La (feat. Sam Smith) : Naughty Boy
1576. Good Thing: Sam Smith
1577. Stay With Me: Sam Smith
1578. I'm Not the Only One: Sam Smith
1579. I've Told You Now: Sam Smith
1580. Like I Can: Sam Smith
1581. Lay Me Down: Sam Smith
1582. Latch: Sam Smith
1583. Restart: Sam Smith
1584. Make It To Me: Sam Smith
1585. Good Thing: Sam Smith
1586. Money On My Mind: Sam Smith
1587. Restart: Sam Smith
1588. Red: Sammy Hagar
1589. I Can't Drive 55: Sammy Hagar

1590. Chevy Van: Sammy Johns
1591. Oye Como Va: Santana
1592. Open Invitation: Santana
1593. No One to Depend On: Santana
1594. Put Your Lights On (feat. Rob Thomas) : Santana
1595. Black Magic Woman: Santana
1596. Angel: Sarah McLachlan
1597. Building A Mystery: Sarah McLachlan
1598. Hold On: Sarah McLachlan
1599. I Will Remember You: Sarah McLachlan
1600. Adia: Sarah McLachlan
1601. Sweet Surrender: Sarah McLachlan
1602. Holiday: Scorpions
1603. Wind of Change: Scorpions
1604. Rock You Like A Hurricane: Scorpions
1605. No One Like You: Scorpions
1606. Rhythm of Love: Scorpions
1607. The Zoo: Scorpions
1608. Send Me An Angel: Scorpions
1609. Still Loving You: Scorpions
1610. Crazy: Seal
1611. Kiss from a Rose: Seal
1612. Deep Water: Seal * *
1613. Fly Like an Eagle: Seal
1614. Get It Together: Seal
1615. Walk On By: Seal
1616. Lips Like Sugar: Seal
1617. Prayer for the Dying: Seal
1618. This Could Be Heaven: Seal

1619. A Change Is Gonna Come: Seal * *

1620. Violet: Seal

1621. Love's Divine: Seal

1622. Padded Cell: Seal

1623. We May Never Pass This Way Again: Seals & Crofts

1624. Diamond Girl: Seals & Crofts

1625. Summer Breeze: Seals & Crofts

1626. Get Closer: Seals & Crofts

1627. Hummingbird: Seals & Crofts

1628. Castles In the Sand: Seals & Crofts

1629. I'll Play for You: Seals & Crofts

1630. East of Ginger Trees: Seals & Crofts

1631. Baby Boy (feat. Beyoncé) : Sean Paul *

1632. I'm Still In Love With You: Sean Paul *

1633. Touch the Sky (feat. DJ Ammo) : Sean Paul *

1634. Temperature: Sean Paul *

1635. Same Old Love: Selena Gomez

1636. Love You Like a Love Song: Selena Gomez & The Scene

1637. Slow Down: Selena Gomez

1638. Come & Get It: Selena Gomez

1639. Sunny Came Home: Shawn Colvin

1640. I Don't Know Why: Shawn Colvin

1641. Stitches: Shawn Mendes

1642. Soak Up the Sun: Sheryl Crow

1643. Steve McQueen: Sheryl Crow

1644. My Favorite Mistake: Sheryl Crow

1645. Sweet Child o' Mine: Sheryl Crow

1646. A Change Would Do You Good: Sheryl Crow

1647. If It Makes You Happy: Sheryl Crow

1648. Everyday Is a Winding Road: Sheryl Crow

1649. All I Wanna Do: Sheryl Crow

1650. Chandelier: Sia

1651. The Greatest: Sia

1652. Electricity (Feat. Diplo & Mark Ronson) : Silk City, Dua Lipa

1653. The Sound of Silence: Simon & Garfunkel

1654. America: Simon & Garfunkel

1655. Scarborough Fair: Simon & Garfunkel

1656. Homeward Bound: Simon & Garfunkel

1657. The 59th Street Bridge Song (Feelin' Groovy) : Simon & Garfunkel

1658. For Emily, Whenever I May Find Her: Simon & Garfunkel

1659. The Boxer: Simon & Garfunkel

1660. El Condor Pasa (If I Could) : Simon & Garfunkel

1661. Bridge Over Troubled Waters: Simon & Garfunkel

1662. Alive and Kicking: Simple Minds

1663. Don't You (Forget About Me) : Simple Minds

1664. Holding Back the Years: Simply Red

1665. Everybody: Sinkane

1666. Everyone: Sinkane

1667. Theme from Life & Livin' It: Sinkane

1668. Favorite Song: Sinkane

1669. Be Here Now: Sinkane

1670. Kiss Them for Me: Siouxsie & The Banshees

1671. Spellbound: Siouxsie & The Banshees

1672. Peek-A-Boo: Siouxsie & The Banshees

1673. The Killing Jar: Siouxsie & The Banshees

1674. The Passenger: Siouxsie & The Banshees

1675. We Are Family: Sister Sledge

1676. Stand Inside Your Love: Smashing Pumpkins

1677. Blood and Roses: The Smithereens

1678. Only A Memory: The Smithereens

1679. How Soon Is Now? : The Smiths

1680. This Charming Man: The Smiths

1681. There Is a Light That Never Goes Out: The Smiths

1682. Cruisin' : Smokey Robinson

1683. Rhythm Is a Dancer: Snap!

1684. The Power: Snap!

1685. Gin and Juice: Snoop Dogg

1686. Sweat: Snoop Dogg & David Guetta

1687. Beautiful (feat. Pharrell & Uncle Charlie Wilson) : Snoop Dogg

1688. Chasing Cars: Snow Patrol

1689. Life On Earth: Snow Patrol

1690. Empress: Snow Patrol

1691. Crack the Shutters: Snow Patrol

1692. Samyaza: the Soil & the Sun

1693. Are You? : the Soil & the Sun

1694. I Know It (I Feel It Too) : the Soil & the Sun

1695. Oiketerion: the Soil & the Sun

1696. Who Is He, Anyway? : the Soil & the Sun

1697. Raised in Glory: the Soil & the Sun

1698. How Long: the Soil & the Sun

1699. She Still Loves Me: SOJA *

1700. Open My Eyes: SOJA *

1701. Lucid Dreams: SOJA *

1702. Rest of My Life: SOJA *

1703. I Believe: SOJA *

1704. Revolution: SOJA * *

1705. I Got You Babe: Sonny & Cher

1706. Black Hole Sun: Soundgarden
1707. Fell On Black Days: Soundgarden
1708. Spoonman: Soundgarden
1709. More Today Than Yesterday: The Spiral Staircase
1710. Nature's Way: Spirit
1711. I Got A Line On You: Spirit
1712. I'll Take You There: The Staple Singers
1713. Respect Yourself: The Staple Singers
1714. Stuck In the Middle With You: Stealers Wheel
1715. Steppin' Out: Steel Pulse *
1716. Worth His Weight in Gold (Rally Round) : Steel Pulse *
1717. Reggae Fever: Steel Pulse *
1718. Chant A Psalm: Steel Pulse *
1719. Any World: Steely Dan
1720. Aja: Steely Dan
1721. Home at Last: Steely Dan
1722. Do It Again: Steely Dan
1723. Any World (That I'm Welcome To) : Steely Dan
1724. Dirty Work: Steely Dan
1725. Pretzel Logic: Steely Dan
1726. Doctor Wu: Steely Dan
1727. Here at the Western World: Steely Dan
1728. Bodhisattva: Steely Dan
1729. Babylon Sisters: Steely Dan
1730. Reelin' In the Years: Steely Dan
1731. Rikki Don't Lose That Number: Steely Dan
1732. Don't Take Me Alive: Steely Dan
1733. Sign In Stranger: Steely Dan
1734. The Royal Scam: Steely Dan

1735. On and On: Stephen Bishop

1736. It Might Be You: Stephen Bishop

1737. Love the One You're With: Stephen Stills

1738. Ecology Song: Stephen Stills

1739. Born to Be Wild: Steppenwolf

1740. Magic Carpet Ride: Steppenwolf

1741. Fly Like an Eagle: Steve Miller Band

1742. Serenade: Steve Miller Band

1743. Rock'n Me: Steve Miller Band

1744. The Stake: Steve Miller Band

1745. Wild Mountain Honey: Steve Miller Band

1746. Jet Airliner: Steve Miller Band

1747. Winter Time: Steve Miller Band

1748. Sugar Babe: Steve Miller Band

1749. Hold On: Steve Winwood

1750. Higher Love: Steve Winwood

1751. While You See A Chance: Steve Winwood

1752. Valerie: Steve Winwood

1753. Roll With It: Steve Winwood

1754. Back In the High Life Again: Steve Winwood

1755. Holding On: Steve Winwood

1756. Arc of a Diver: Steve Winwood

1757. Bella Donna: Stevie Nicks

1758. After the Glitter Fades: Stevie Nicks

1759. Edge of Seventeen: Stevie Nicks

1760. Leather and Lace: Stevie Nicks and Don Henley

1761. Stand Back: Stevie Nicks

1762. Bella Donna: Stevie Nicks

1763. Kind of Woman: Stevie Nicks

1764. After the Glitter Fades: Stevie Nicks
1765. Think About It: Stevie Nicks
1766. Edge of Seventeen: Stevie Nicks
1767. Stop Draggin' My Heart Around: Stevie Nicks & Tom Petty
1768. Leather & Lace: Stevie Nicks & Don Henley
1769. Sleeping Angel: Stevie Nicks
1770. If You Were My Love: Stevie Nicks
1771. Angel: Stevie Nicks
1772. Stand Back: Stevie Nicks
1773. Boogie On Reggae Woman: Stevie Wonder
1774. Superstition: Stevie Wonder
1775. Golden Lady: Stevie Wonder
1776. Higher Ground: Stevie Wonder
1777. Living For the City: Stevie Wonder
1778. That Girl: Stevie Wonder
1779. Isn't She Lovely: Stevie Wonder
1780. Long May You Run: The Stills-Young Band
1781. Fields of Gold: Sting
1782. Desert Rose: Sting
1783. Brand New Day: Sting
1784. After the Rain Has Fallen: Sting
1785. Be Still My Beating Heart: Sting
1786. Vaseline: Stone Temple Pilots
1787. You're the Best Thing: The Style Council
1788. Betcha by Golly, Wow: The Stylistics
1789. Lady: Styx
1790. Crystal Ball: Styx
1791. Light Up: Styx
1792. Lorelei: Styx

1793. Suite Madame Blue: Styx * *

1794. You Need Love: Styx

1795. Fooling Yourself: Styx

1796. Come Sail Away: Styx

1797. Man In the Wilderness: Styx

1798. Renegade: Styx

1799. Blue Collar Man: Styx

1800. The Grand Illusion: Styx

1801. Santeria: Sublime

1802. What I Got: Sublime

1803. Rapper's Delight: The Sugarhill Gang

1804. Give a Little Bit: Supertramp

1805. Dreamer: Supertramp

1806. Take the Long Way Home: Supertramp

1807. I Hear A Symphony: The Supremes

1808. You Can't Hurry Love: The Supremes

1809. Baby Love: The Supremes

1810. Someday We'll Be Together: The Supremes

1811. Come See About Me: The Supremes

1812. River Deep, Mountain High: The Supremes & Four Tops

1813. Eye of the Tiger: Survivor

1814. The Ballroom Blitz: The Sweet

1815. Fox On the Run: The Sweet

1816. Boogie Fever: The Sylvers

1817. Once In a Lifetime: Talking Heads

1818. And She Was: Talking Heads

1819. (Nothing But) Flowers: Talking Heads

1820. Burning Down the House: Talking Heads

1821. Take Me to the River: Talking Heads

1822. Talk Talk: Talk Talk
1823. Let It Happen: Tame Impala
1824. The Moment: Tame Impala
1825. Eventually: Tame Impala
1826. Disciples: Tame Impala
1827. Reality In Motion: Tame Impala
1828. Patience: Tame Impala
1829. Slide Through My Fingers: Tame Impala
1830. Larger Than Life: Tarrus Riley * *
1831. If It's Jah Will: Tarrus Riley *
1832. Paradise: Tarrus Riley *
1833. Eye Sight: Tarrus Riley *
1834. Whispers: Tarrus Riley * *
1835. Stay With You: Tarrus Riley *
1836. Let Love Live (feat. Duane Stephenson) : Tarrus Riley * *
1837. Family (feat. Della Manly) : Tarrus Riley *
1838. Boogie Oogie Oogie: A Taste of Honey
1839. Love Story: Taylor Swift
1840. Fifteen: Taylor Swift
1841. Mean: Taylor Swift
1842. Our Song: Taylor Swift
1843. Style: Taylor Swift
1844. Mad World: Tears for Fears
1845. Pale Shelter: Tears for Fears
1846. Suffer the Children: Tears for Fears
1847. Raoul and the Kings of Spain: Tears for Fears
1848. Shout: Tears for Fears
1849. Everybody Wants to Rule the World: Tears for Fears
1850. Head Over Heels: Tears for Fears

1851. Just My Imagination: The Temptations
1852. My Girl: The Temptations
1853. Ain't Too Proud to Beg: The Temptations
1854. Papa Was a Rollin' Stone: The Temptations
1855. I Can't Get Next to You: The Temptations
1856. I Wish It Would Rain: The Temptations
1857. Happy People: The Temptations
1858. Because the Night: 10,000 Maniacs
1859. What's the Matter Here: 10,000 Maniacs
1860. Hey Jack Kerouac: 10,000 Maniacs
1861. Like the Weather: 10,000 Maniacs
1862. These Are Days: 10,000 Maniacs
1863. Gold Rush Brides: 10,000 Maniacs
1864. More Than This: 10,000 Maniacs
1865. Candy Everybody Wants: 10,000 Maniacs
1866. Trouble Me: 10,000 Maniacs
1867. Jezebel: 10,000 Maniacs
1868. Sign Your Name: Terence Trent D'Arby
1869. Wishing Well: Terence Trent D'Arby
1870. Signs: Tesla
1871. The Boys Are Back in Town: Thin Lizzy
1872. Semi-Charmed Life: Third Eye Blind
1873. Now That We Found Love: Third World *
1874. Try Jah Love: Third World *
1875. Freedom Must be Now (feat. Michael Rose) : Third World *
1876. Reggae Ambassador: Third World *
1877. Prisoner in the Street: Third World *
1878. Jah Glory: Third World *
1879. Irie Ites: Third World *

1880. Sense of Purpose: Third World *
1881. Rhythm of Life: Third World *
1882. Cool Meditation: Third World *
1883. Uptown Rebel: Third World *
1884. Always Around: Third World *
1885. Loving You Is Easy: Third World *
1886. Rockin' Into the Night: 38 Special
1887. Hold On Loosely: 38 Special
1888. Fantasy Girl: 38 Special
1889. She Blinded Me With Science: Thomas Dolby
1890. Lay Your Hands On Me: Thompson Twins
1891. Hold Me Now: Thompson Twins
1892. Mama Told Me (Not to Come) : Three Dog Night
1893. Shambala; Three Dog Night
1894. Black and White: Three Dog Night
1895. Celebrate: Three Dog Night
1896. Paradise: Through the Roots *
1897. Here to Stay: Through the Roots *
1898. Bear With Me (feat. Eric Rachmany) : Through the Roots *
1899. On This Vibe: Through the Roots *
1900. Voices Carry: 'Til Tuesday
1901. New Vision: Title Fight
1902. Something's Always Wrong: Toad the Wet Sprocket
1903. Hello It's Me: Todd Rundgren
1904. Free Fallin': Tom Petty
1905. Refugee: Tom Petty & The Heartbreakers
1906. Here Comes My Girl: Tom Petty & The Heartbreakers
1907. Even the Losers: Tom Petty & The Heartbreakers
1908. You Tell Me: Tom Petty & The Heartbreakers

1909. Louisiana Rain: Tom Petty & The Heartbreakers
1910. Breakdown: Tom Petty & The Heartbreakers
1911. American Girl: Tom Petty & The Heartbreakers
1912. I Need to Know: Tom Petty & The Heartbreakers
1913. Mary Jane's Last Dance: Tom Petty & The Heartbreakers
1914. Un-Break My Heart: Toni Braxton
1915. Hey Jupiter: Tori Amos
1916. Cornflake Girl: Tori Amos
1917. Africa: Toto
1918. Hold the Line: Toto
1919. Rosanna: Toto
1920. Heaven's Here On Earth: Tracy Chapman
1921. Fast Car: Tracy Chapman
1922. Give Me One Reason: Tracy Chapman
1923. Talkin' Bout a Revolution: Tracy Chapman * *
1924. Across the Lines: Tracy Chapman
1925. Stand By Me: Tracy Chapman
1926. The Promise: Tracy Chapman
1927. Crossroads: Tracy Chapman
1928. All That You Have Is Your Soul: Tracy Chapman
1929. New Beginning: Tracy Chapman
1930. John Barleycorn (Must Die) : Traffic
1931. Dear Mr. Fantasy: Traffic
1932. Empty Pages: Traffic
1933. Feelin' Alright? : Traffic
1934. The Low Spark of High-Heeled Boys: Traffic
1935. Heaven Is In Your Mind: Traffic
1936. Drops of Jupiter: Train
1937. Calling All Angels: Train

1938. Drive By: Train
1939. Disco Inferno: The Trammps
1940. Immigrant Song: Trent Reznor & Atticus Ross & Karen O
1941. Nobody Else But You: Trey Songz
1942. The Garden: Tribal Seeds *
1943. All I Know: Tribal Seeds *
1944. Stillness of Night: Tribal Seeds *
1945. Love Psalm: Tribal Seeds *
1946. Beautiful Mysterious: Tribal Seeds *
1947. Walkaway Joe: Trisha Yearwood
1948. Hold On: Triumph
1949. Lay It On the Line: Triumph
1950. Somebody's Out There: Triumph
1951. California Love (feat. Roger Troutman & Dr. Dre) : 2Pac
1952. Keep Ya Head Up: 2Pac * *
1953. Dear Mama: 2Pac
1954. Changes (feat. Talent) : 2Pac
1955. Happy Together: The Turtles
1956. Heathens: twenty one pilots
1957. Level of Concern: twenty one pilots
1958. Sunday Bloody Sunday: U2 * *
1959. Where the Streets Have No Name: U2
1960. New Year's Day: U2
1961. Mysterious Ways: U2
1962. I Will Follow: U2
1963. Bullet the Blue Sky: U2
1964. In God's Country: U2
1965. Trip Through Your Wires: U2
1966. Desire: U2

1967. I Still Haven't Found What I'm Looking For: U2
1968. Pride (In the Name of Love) : U2
1969. The Miracle (Of Joey Ramone) : U2
1970. California (There Is No End to Love) : U2
1971. Cedarwood Road: U2
1972. Beautiful Day: U2
1973. Many Rivers to Cross: UB40 *
1974. (I Can't Help) Falling In Love with You: UB40 *
1975. Red Red Wine: UB40 *
1976. Here I Am (Come and Take Me) : UB40 *
1977. I Got You Babe: UB40 *
1978. The Way You Do the Things You Do: UB40 *
1979. Groovin' (Out On Life) : UB40 *
1980. Breakfast In Bed: UB40 & Chrissie Hynde *
1981. Swing Low (feat. The United Colours of Sound) : UB40 *
1982. Lights Out: UFO
1983. Love to Love: UFO
1984. Rock Bottom: UFO
1985. Yeah! (feat. Lil Jon & Ludacris) : Usher
1986. You Make Me Wanna… : Usher
1987. U Remind Me: Usher
1988. Omg (feat. will.i.am) : Usher
1989. Superstar: Usher
1990. Caught Up: Usher
1991. Without You (feat. Usher) : David Guetta
1992. Ain't Talkin' 'Bout Love: Van Halen
1993. Dance the Night Away: Van Halen
1994. Runnin' with the Devil: Van Halen
1995. And the Cradle Will Rock… : Van Halen

1996. Panama: Van Halen
1997. When It's Love: Van Halen
1998. You Really Got Me: Van Halen
1999. Jamie's Cryin' : Van Halen
2000. Feel Your Love Tonight: Van Halen
2001. Beautiful Girls: Van Halen
2002. Best of Both Worlds: Van Halen
2003. Tupelo Honey: Van Morrison
2004. Sweet Thing: Van Morrison
2005. Brown Eyed Girl: Van Morrison
2006. Gloria (feat. Van Morrison) : Them
2007. Crazy Love: Van Morrison
2008. Have I Told You Lately: Van Morrison
2009. Domino: Van Morrison
2010. And It Stoned Me: Van Morrison
2011. Caravan: Van Morrison
2012. Into the Mystic: Van Morrison
2013. Glad Tidings: Van Morrison
2014. Jackie Wilson Said (I'm In Heaven When You Smile) : Van Morrison
2015. Wonderful Remark: Van Morrison
2016. Full Force Gale: Van Morrison
2017. Bitter Sweet Symphony: The Verve
2018. All the Stars: The Wailin' Jennys
2019. Swing Low Sail High: The Wailin' Jennys
2020. Bright Morning Stars: The Wailin' Jennys
2021. Mexican Radio: Wall of Voodoo
2022. Magnet and Steel: Walter Egan
2023. Dance Hall Days: Wang Chung
2024. Everybody Have Fun Tonight: Wang Chung

2025. To Live And Die In L.A. : Wang Chung
2026. Glad You Came: The Wanted
2027. Raw Evolution: Warbly Jets
2028. It's Raining Men; The Weather Girls
2029. Alone Again: The Weeknd
2030. Blinding Lights: The Weeknd
2031. Too Late: The Weeknd
2032. Hardest To Love: The Weeknd
2033. Faith: The Weeknd
2034. In Your Eyes: The Weeknd
2035. Save Your Tears: The Weeknd
2036. Can't Feel My Face: The Weeknd
2037. Starboy (feat. Daft Punk) : The Weeknd
2038. Love To Lay: The Weeknd
2039. Nothing Compares: The Weeknd
2040. I Feel It Coming (feat. Daft Punk) : The Weeknd
2041. Love Me Harder: Ariana Grande & The Weeknd
2042. Happy Hour: Weezer
2043. Island In the Sun: Weezer
2044. When the Children Cry: White Lion * *
2045. Seven Nation Army: The White Stripes
2046. Here I Go Again: Whitesnake
2047. Still of the Night: Whitesnake
2048. Eminence Front: The Who
2049. Love, Reign O'er Me: The Who
2050. Baba O'Riley: The Who
2051. Won't Get Fooled Again: The Who
2052. Who Are You: The Who
2053. Behind Blue Eyes: The Who

2054. I Can See For Miles: The Who
2055. Magic Bus: The Who
2056. Join Together: The Who
2057. The Seeker: The Who
2058. Play That Funky Music: Wild Cherry
2059. S.O.S. (Mother Nature) : will.i.am * *
2060. Hold On: Wilson Phillips
2061. Divine Sorrow (feat. Avicii) : Wyclef Jean
2062. If You Should See: Wye Oak
2063. Renegades: X Ambassadors
2064. Summertime Girls: Y & T
2065. Situation: Yaz
2066. Roundabout: Yes
2067. Long Distance Runaround: Yes
2068. I've Seen All Good People: Yes
2069. Faraway Look: Yola
2070. Shady Grove: Yola
2071. Ride Out In the Country: Yola
2072. Walk Through Fire: Yola
2073. Rock Me Gently: Yola
2074. Love All Night: Yola
2075. Love Is Light: Yola
2076. Groovin' : The Young Rascals
2077. Get Together: The Youngbloods
2078. Clarity (feat. Foxes) : Zedd
2079. Happy Now (feat. Elley Duhe)
2080. Dragonfly: Ziggy Marley *
2081. I Get Out: Ziggy Marley *
2082. True to Myself: Ziggy Marley *

2083. In the Name of God: Ziggy Marley * *

2084. Rainbow In the Sky: Ziggy Marley *

2085. Good Old Days: Ziggy Marley *

2086. DYKL (Don't You Kill Love) : Ziggy Marley *

2087. Higher Vibrations: Ziggy Marley * *

2088. Personal Revolution: Ziggy Marley *

2089. Welcome to the World: Ziggy Marley *

2090. Jah Will Be Done: Ziggy Marley *

2091. Tomorrow People: Ziggy Marley *

2092. Changes: Ziggy Marley *

2093. Conscious Party: Ziggy Marley *

2094. Time of the Season: The Zombies

2095. Cheap Sunglasses: ZZ Top

2096. Sharp Dressed Man: ZZ Top

2097. Tush: ZZ Top

2098. La Grange: ZZ Top

2099. Gimme All Your Lovin' : ZZ Top

2100. I Thank You: ZZ Top

RESOURCES FOR INSIGHT:

It would be impossible for me to include all the resources that have helped me, but here is a start:

(Alphabetical, by title)

A New Earth: Eckhart Tolle

Abraham-Hicks: https://www.abraham-hicks.com

Abraham-Hicks: YouTube

An Ascension Handbook: Tony Stubbs

An Unquiet Mind: Kay Redfield Jamison

Anatomy of the Spirit: Carolyn Myss

The Artist's Way: Julia Cameron

Ask and It Is Given: Esther and Jerry Hicks

Ask Your Guides: Sonia Choquette

Bird by Bird: Anne Lamotte

Breethe: the app

Chicken Soup for the Soul: Jack Canfield & Mark Victor Hansen

Cosmic Messengers: Elizabeth Peru

Creative Visualization: Shakti Gawain

Discovering Your Personality Type: Don Richard Riso and Russ Hudson

Dry. : Augusten Burroughs

Eat Pray Love: Elizabeth Gilbert

Feeling Good: David D. Burns, M.D.

Getting In the Gap: Dr. Wayne W. Dyer

Girl, Interrupted: Susanna Kaysen

Giving Back: Bert Berkeley, Peter Economy

Giving: Bill Clinton

God Is No Laughing Matter: Julia Cameron

Handbook to Higher Consciousness: The Science of Happiness: Ken Keyes, Jr.

How to Get What You Want and Want What You Have: John Gray

Journey of Your Soul: Shepherd Hoodwin

Leave Your Mind Behind: Matthew McKay, Ph.D and Catharine Suther

Living in the Light: Shakti Gawain

Living Loving and Learning: Leo Buscaglia, Ph. D.

Opening to Channel: How to Connect With Your Guide: Sanaya Roman and Duane Packer

101 Things I Wish I Knew When I Got Married: Linda and Charlie Bloom

Peace Is Every Step: Thich Nhat Hanh

Poetry: A Pocket Anthology: R. S. Gwynn

Postcards from the Edge: Carrie Fisher

Real Magic: Dr. Wayne W. Dyer

Seth Speaks: Jane Roberts

Siddhartha: Herman Hesse

Spark Joy: Kondo

Spiritual Growth: Being Your High Self: Sanaya Roman

Spiritual Madness: Carolyn Myss

10% Happier: the app

10 Secrets for Success and Inner Peace: Dr. Wayne W. Dyer

The Angelic Origins of the Soul: Discovering Your Divine Purpose: Tricia McCannon

The Bell Jar: Sylvia Plath

The Best Awful: Carrie Fisher

The Book of Questions: Gregory Stoch, Ph.D.

The Celestine Prophecy: James Redfield

The Confident Woman: Marjorie Hansen Shaevitz

The Evolutionary Empath: A Practical Guide for Heart-Centered Consciousness: Rev. Stephanie Red Feather, Ph.D.

The Four Agreements: Don Miguel Ruiz

The Four Levels of Healing: Shakti Gawain

The Generosity Network: Jennifer McCrea and Jeffrey C. Walker

The Happiness Project: Gretchen Rubin

The Holy Bible

The Impossible Will Take A Little While: A Citizen's Guide to Hope in a Time of Fear: Paul Rogat Loeb

The Lively Art of Writing: Lucile Vaughan Payne

The Magic of Thinking Big: David J. Schwartz, Ph.D.

The Money Class: Suze Orman

The Power Is Within You: Louise Haye

The Power of Intention: Dr. Wayne W. Dyer

The Power of Now: Eckhart Tolle

The Purpose of Your Life: Carol Adrienne

The Qur'an

The Right to Write: Julia Cameron

The Seat of the Soul: Gary Zukav

The Seven Spiritual Laws of Success: Deepak Chopra

The Teaching of Buddha: Buddhist Promoting Foundation: Japan

There's a Spiritual Solution to Every Problem: Dr. Wayne Dyer

Walking In This World: Julia Cameron

Where Are You Going? A Guide to the Spiritual Journey:
    Swami Muktananda

Why People Don't Heal and How They Can: Carolyn Myss, Ph.D.

Working with Chakras for Belief Change: Nikki Gresham-Record

You Can Heal Your Life: Louise Haye

RESOURCES FOR SUPPORT

National Alliance on Mental Illness: http://www.nami.org

Depression and Bipolar Disorder Support Alliance: dbsalliance.org

My Depression Team: mydepressionteam.com

Anxiety and Depression Association of America: adaa.org

Psycom: psycom.net

Choices in Recovery: choicesinrecovery.com

National Network of Depression Centers: nndc.org/resource-links

National Institute for Mental Health Shareable Resources on Depression: http://www.nimh.nih.gov/health/education-awareness/shareable-resources-on-depression.shtml

Medline Plus: medlineplus.gov

Mental Help: mentalhelp.net

Mental Health.gov: mentalhealth.gov/get-help

Association for Behavioral and Cognitive Therapies: abct.org/Home/

Healthy Place: healthyplace.com

Healthline: Support for your Mental Health: healthline.com

Ask Hopkins Psychiatry: askhopkinspsychiatry.org

Massachusetts General MADI Resource Center: massgeneral.org/psychiatry/about/patient-education

Mayo Clinic Patient Information:

mayoclinic.org/patient-care-and-health-information

American Psychiatric Association Foundation: apafdn.org

Brain and Behavior Research Foundation: bbrfoundation.org

Project Hope and Beyond: community.projecthopeandbeyond.com

Group Beyond Blue: Facebook.com/groups/groupbeyondblue/

Families for Depression Awareness: familyaware.org

Befrienders Worldwide: befrienders.org

To Write Love on Her Arms: twloha.com

American Association of Suicidology: suicidology.org

MULTICULTURAL RESOURCES FOR SUPPORT

National Asian American Pacific Islander Mental Health Association: naapimha.org

Asian American Psychological Association: aapaonline.org

National Asian Pacific American Families Against Substance Abuse: napafasa.org

Office of Minority Mental Health – United States: minorityhealth.hhs.gov/Default.aspx

Black Mental Health Alliance: blackmentalhealth.com

The Association of Black Psychologists: abpsi.org

Ourselves Black: ourselvesblack.com

Black Girls Smile: blackgirlssmile.org

Black Girl Mental Health: blackgirlmentalhealth.tumblr.com

Latino Mental Health – NAMI: nami.org/Your-Journey/Identity-and-Cultural-Dimensions/Hispanic-Latinx

American Society of Hispanic Psychiatry: americansocietyhispanicpsychiatry.com

Association of Hispanic Mental Health Professionals: ahmhp.org/home/index.php

National Latino Behavioral Health Association: nlbha.org

RESOURCES FOR SUPPORT IN A CRISIS

National Suicide Prevention Lifeline: 1-800-273- TALK (8255)

TTY: 1-800-799-4TTY (4889)

National Alliance on Mental Illness (NAMI) Hotline: 1-800-950-NAMI (6264)

or info@nami.org (M-F 10 AM – 8 PM EST)

Crisis Hotline: text: Text NAMI to 741741 (24/7 support)

Veteran Crisis Line: 1-800-273-8255 (Press "1") (24/7 support)

Suicide Hotline by State: suicide.org/suicide-hotlines.html

International Suicide Hotline: suicide.org/international-suicide-hotlines.html

National Domestic Violence Hotline: 1-800-799-SAFE (7233) (24/7 support)

National Sexual Assault Hotline: 1-800-656-HOPE (4673) (24/7 support)